The Facts On File
JUNIOR
VISUAL
DICTIONARY

D0123227

CIP data available on request from publisher.

Original edition in English :
Copyright © 1989 by Éditions Québec/Amérique Inc.

Published under licence in the United States of America by :
Facts On File, Inc.
460 Park Avenue South
New York NY 10016
USA

ISBN : 0-8160-2222-4

Printed and bound in Canada

This book was produced on a Macintosh computer from Apple Computer Inc.

The Facts On File
JUNIOR
VISUAL
DICTIONARY

JEAN-CLAUDE CORBEIL
ARIANE ARCHAMBAULT

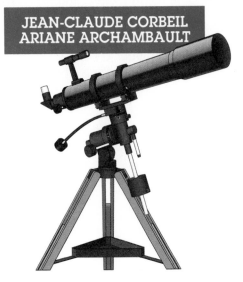

Director of Computer Graphics:
François Fortin

Art Director:
Jean-Louis Martin

Computer Graphic Artists:
**Jacques Perrault,
Benoît Bourdeau,
Anne Tremblay**

Computer Copy Editing:
Anik Lapointe

Facts On File
New York • Oxford

THEMES AND SUBJECTS

Cassette recorder............86
Cassette player............86
Camera............................87

1

STARTING FROM THE LIST OF THEMES AND SUBJECTS

The list of themes and subjects (pages 6 and 7) lists every topic of interest in the dictionary and specifies the page where you will find the corresponding picture.

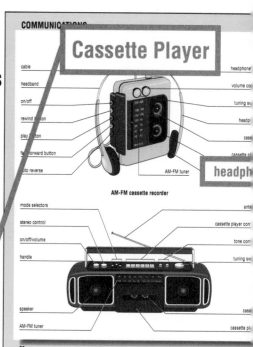

COMMUNICATIONS

Cassette Player

cable

headband

on/off

rewind button

play button

fast forward button

auto reverse

headphone

volume co

tuning sw

headp

cass

cassette pl

headph

AM-FM tuner

AM-FM cassette recorder

mode selectors

stereo control

on/off/volume

handle

speaker

AM-FM tuner

ante

cassette player con

tone con

tuning sw

cass

cassette pl

86

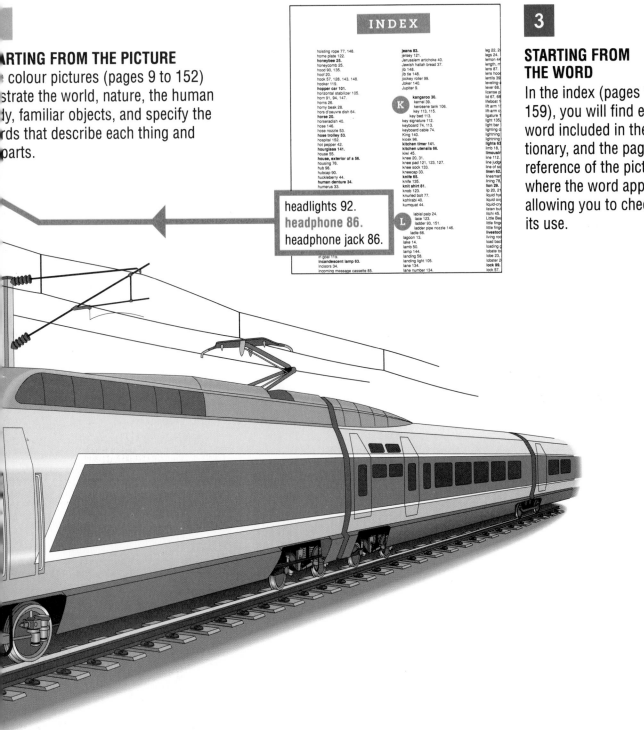

RTING FROM THE PICTURE

e colour pictures (pages 9 to 152) strate the world, nature, the human dy, familiar objects, and specify the rds that describe each thing and parts.

3

STARTING FROM THE WORD

In the index (pages 153 to 159), you will find every word included in the dictionary, and the page reference of the picture where the word appears, allowing you to check its use.

INDEX

hoisting rope 77, 148.
home plate 122.
honeybee 25.
honeycomb 25.
hood 90, 135.
hoof 20.
hook 57, 128, 143, 148.
hooker 119.
hopper car 101.
horizontal stabilizer 105.
horn 91, 94, 147.
horns 26.
horny beak 28.
hors d'oeuvre dish 64.
horse 20.
horseradish 40.
hose 146.
hose nozzle 53.
hose trolley 53.
hospital 152.
hot pepper 42.
hourglass 141.
house 55.
house, exterior of a 56.
housing 76.
hub 98.
hubcap 90.
huckleberry 44.
human denture 34.
humerus 33.

headlights 92.
headphone 86.
headphone jack 86.

in goal 119.
incandescent lamp 63.
incisors 34.
incoming message cassette 85.

jeans 83.
jersey 121.
Jerusalem artichoke 40.
Jewish hallah bread 37.
jib 148.
jib tie 148.
jockey roller 99.
Joker 140.
Jupiter 9.

K   **kangaroo 30.**
kernel 39.
kerosene tank 106.
key 113, 115.
key bed 113.
key signature 112.
keyboard 74, 113.
keyboard cable 74.
King 140.
kiosk 96.
kitchen timer 141.
kitchen utensils 66.
kiwi 45.
knee 20, 31.
knee pad 121, 123, 127.
knee sock 133.
kneecap 33.
knife 135.
knit shirt 81.
knob 123.
knurled bolt 77.
kohlrabi 40.
kumquat 44.

L   labial palp 24.
lace 123.
ladder 93, 151.
ladder pipe nozzle 146.
ladle 66.
lagoon 13.
lake 14.
lamb 50.
lamp 144.
landing 58.
landing light 105.
lane 134.
lane number 134.

leg 22, 2
legs 24.
lemon 44
length, m
lens 87.
lens hoo
lentils 39
leveling-s
lever 68.
license p
lid 67, 68
lifeboat 1
lift arm 1
lift-arm c
ligature c
light 135.
light bar
lighting c
lightning
lightning
lights 63
limb 18.
limousin
line 112.
line judge
line of sc
linen 62.
linesman
lining 78,
lion 29.
lip 20, 21
liquid hy
liquid oxi
liquid-cry
listen but
litchi 45.
Little Bea
little finge
little finge
livestoc
living roo
load bac
loading g
lobate to
lobe 23,
lobster 2
lock 99.
lock 57.

THEMES AND SUBJECTS

ANIMAL KINGDOM

Horse...20
Dog..21
Cat..21
Bird...22
Butterfly......................................24
Honeybee and hive..............................25
Lobster..26
Snail..26
Fish...27
Frog...27
Turtle...28
Venomous snake.................................28
Wild animals...................................29

ARCHITECTURE

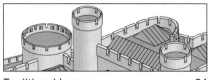

Traditional houses.............................54
Castle...55

CLOTHING

Running shoe...................................78
Men's clothing.................................79
Sweaters.......................................81
Women's clothing...............................82
Children's clothing............................83
Personal articles..............................84

COMMUNICATIONS

Telephone set..................................85
Cassette recorder..............................86
Cassette player................................86
Camera...87
Slide projector................................87
Television set.................................88
Video tape recorder............................88
Sound reproducing system.......................89
Video camera...................................89

DO-IT-YOURSELF

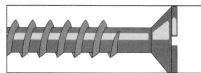

Carpentry......................................75
Tools..76
Painting upkeep................................77

EARTH

Continents.....................................12
Coastal features...............................13
Volcano..13
Cave...14
Mountain.......................................14
Weather..15

FARM

Farmstead......................................49
Farm's animals.................................50

FOOD

Bread..37
Vegetables.....................................38
Fruits...43
Nuts...46
Cheeses..47
Desserts.......................................48

GARDENING

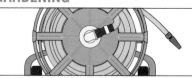

Pleasure garden................................51
Tools and equipment............................52

HEAVY MACHINERY

Fire engines...................................146
Cranes...148
Bulldozer......................................149
Wheel loader...................................150
Dump truck.....................................151
Hydraulic shovel...............................151

HOUSE

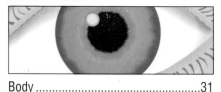

Exterior of a house............................56
Door and window................................57
Stairs...58
Bathroom.......................................59
Chair and table................................60
Armchairs......................................61
Bed and linen..................................62
Lights...63
Dinnerware.....................................64
Silverware.....................................65
Kitchen utensils...............................66
Cooking utensils...............................67
Domestic appliances............................68
Electric range.................................69
Refrigerator...................................70

HUMAN BODY

Body...31
Skeleton.......................................33
Mouth and teeth................................34
Ear..35
Eye..35
Hand...36
Nose...36

THEMES AND SUBJECTS

MEASURING DEVICES

Measure of time..................................141
Measure of weight..............................142
Measure of distance 143
Measure of length...............................143
Measure of pressure..........................143
Measure of temperature 143

MUSIC

Musical notation 112
Upright piano......................................113
Classical guitar 114
Violin 114
Saxophone..115
Trumpet 115
Drums 116
Electric guitar 116
Symphony orchestra 117

OPTICAL INSTRUMENTS

Binocular microscope..........................144
Reflecting telescope 145
Refracting telescope 145

SCHOOL

Plane surfaces, solids and colors 71
School supplies 72
Microcomputer......................................74
Pocket calculator 74

SKY

Planets of the solar system 9
Phases of the Moon.............................10
Sun...10
Comet...11
Stars...11

SPORTS

Soccer 118
Rugby 119
Football..120
Baseball 122
Cricket 124
Hockey...125
Ice hockey 126
Skating 128
Basketball 129
Tennis 130
Alpine skiing 132
Cross-country skiing 133
Diving 134
Swimming 134
Skin diving...135
Sailboard 136
Camping 137
Bow 139
Dart and dartboard 139
Indoor games 140

SYMBOLS

Major road signs 152
Public signs 152

TRANSPORTS

Road transport
Automobile 90
Caravan 93
Truck trailer 94
Motorcycle...95
Service station.....................................96
Bridges 97
Bicycle 98
Rail transport
High-speed train 100
Locomotive..100
Types of cars 101
Maritime transport
Passenger liner...................................102
Submarine 103
Air transport
Long-range jet 104
Helicopter..105
Space travel
Rocket 106
Space shuttle.......................................107

VEGETABLE KINGDOM

Parts of a plant 16
Parts of a leaf 17
Parts of a flower..................................17
Parts of a tree 18
Parts of a mushroom...........................19

WEAPONS

Armor 108
Swords and daggers............................109
Crossbow 109
Pistol 110
Revolver 110
Tank..111

planets of the solar system

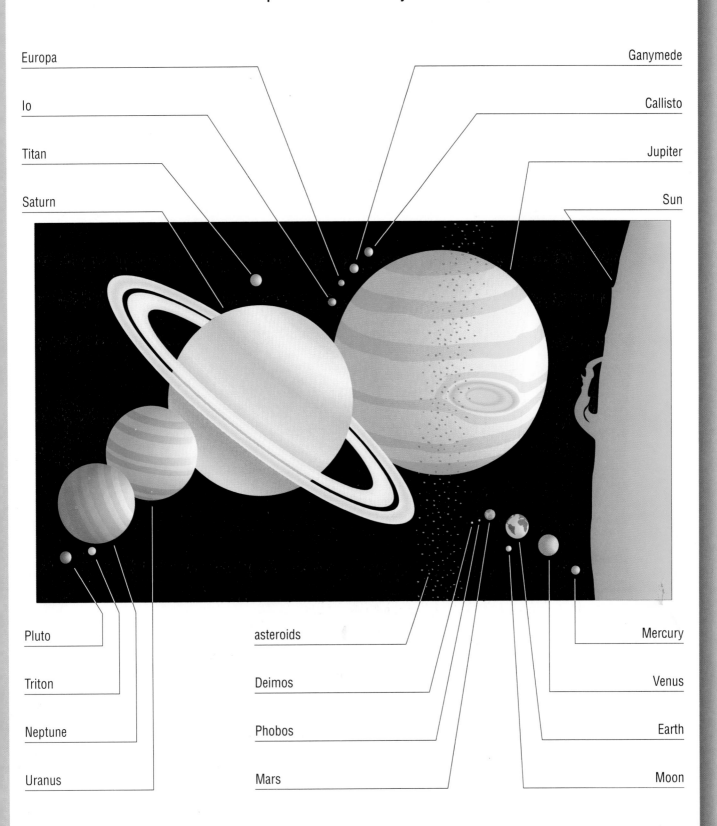

Europa

Ganymede

Io

Callisto

Titan

Jupiter

Saturn

Sun

Pluto

asteroids

Mercury

Triton

Deimos

Venus

Neptune

Phobos

Earth

Uranus

Mars

Moon

Sun

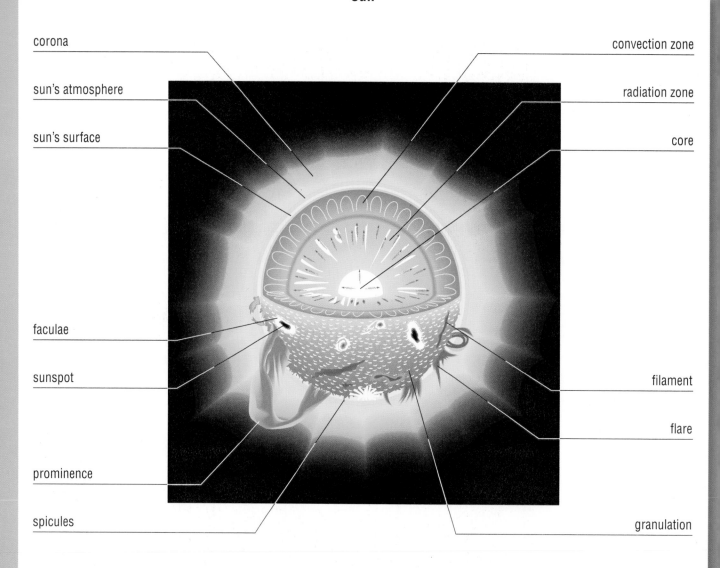

corona

sun's atmosphere

sun's surface

faculae

sunspot

prominence

spicules

convection zone

radiation zone

core

filament

flare

granulation

phases of the Moon

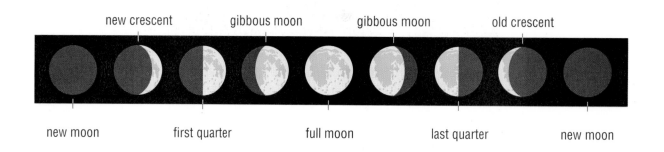

new crescent

gibbous moon

gibbous moon

old crescent

new moon

first quarter

full moon

last quarter

new moon

comet

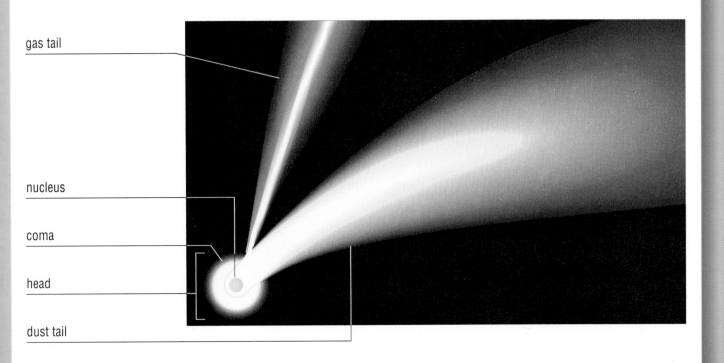

gas tail

nucleus

coma

head

dust tail

stars

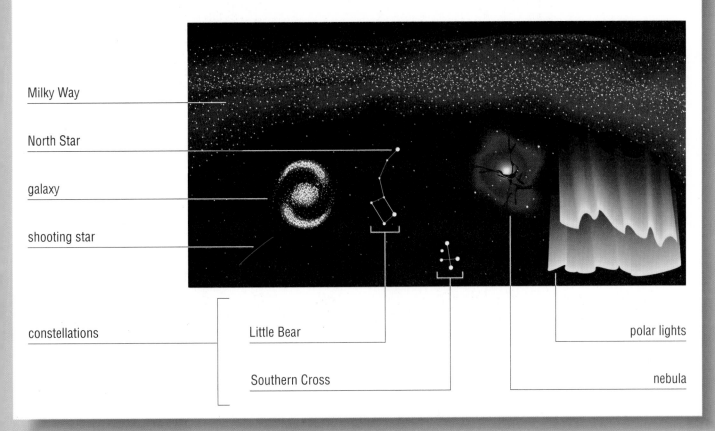

Milky Way

North Star

galaxy

shooting star

constellations

Little Bear

Southern Cross

polar lights

nebula

EARTH

continents

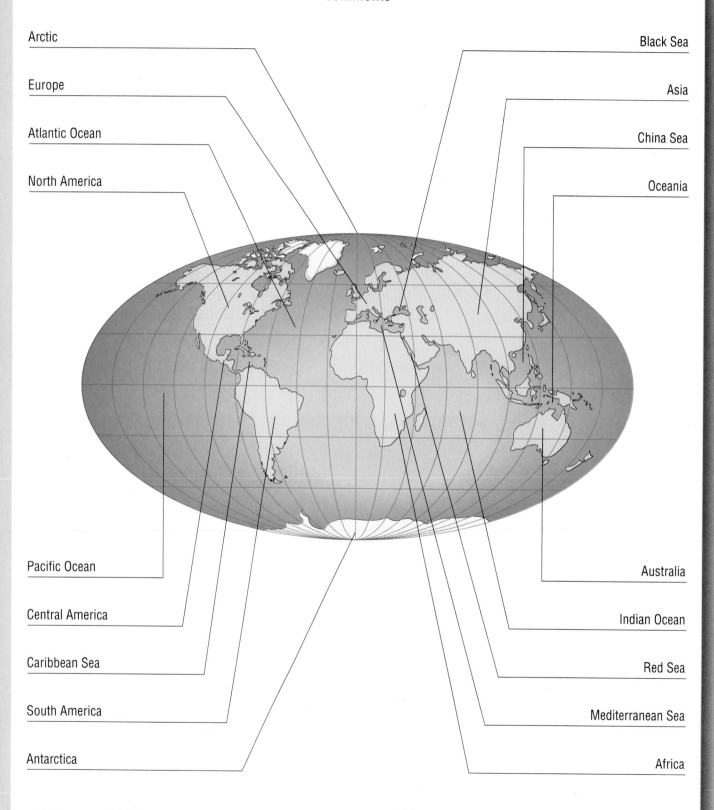

Arctic

Europe

Atlantic Ocean

North America

Pacific Ocean

Central America

Caribbean Sea

South America

Antarctica

Black Sea

Asia

China Sea

Oceania

Australia

Indian Ocean

Red Sea

Mediterranean Sea

Africa

volcano

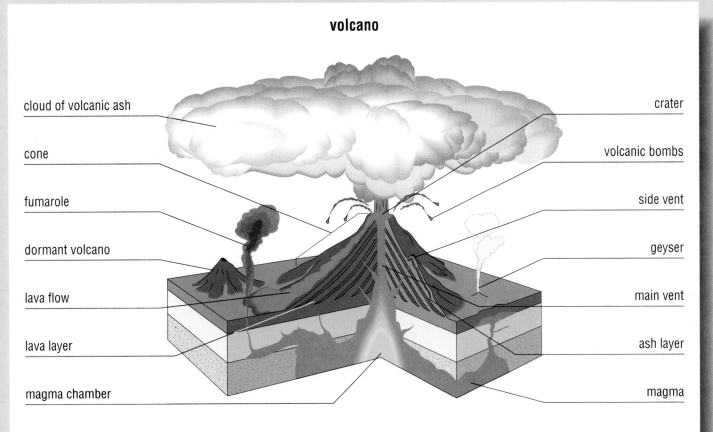

cloud of volcanic ash

cone

fumarole

dormant volcano

lava flow

lava layer

magma chamber

crater

volcanic bombs

side vent

geyser

main vent

ash layer

magma

coastal features

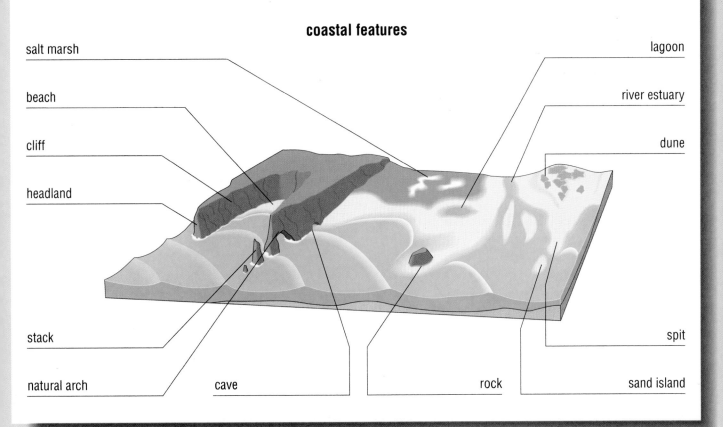

salt marsh

beach

cliff

headland

stack

natural arch

cave

rock

lagoon

river estuary

dune

spit

sand island

EARTH

mountain

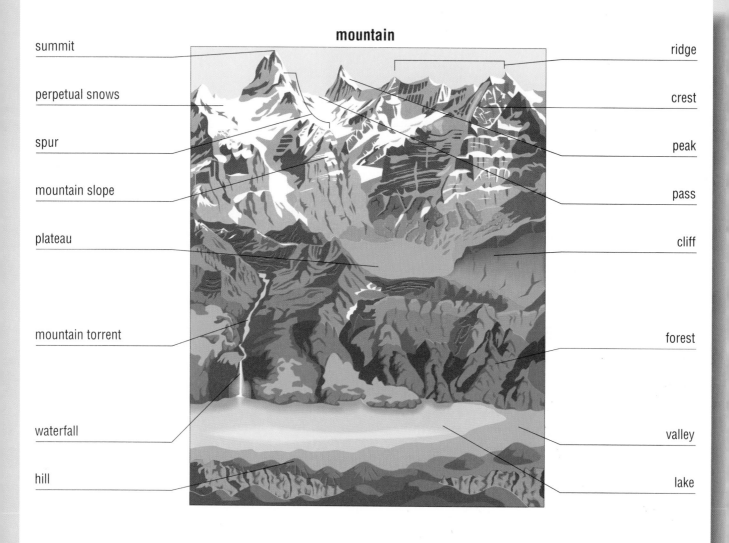

summit

perpetual snows

spur

mountain slope

plateau

mountain torrent

waterfall

hill

ridge

crest

peak

pass

cliff

forest

valley

lake

cave

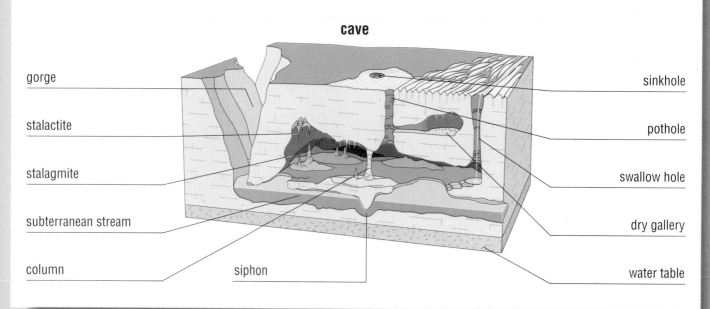

gorge

stalactite

stalagmite

subterranean stream

column

siphon

sinkhole

pothole

swallow hole

dry gallery

water table

weather

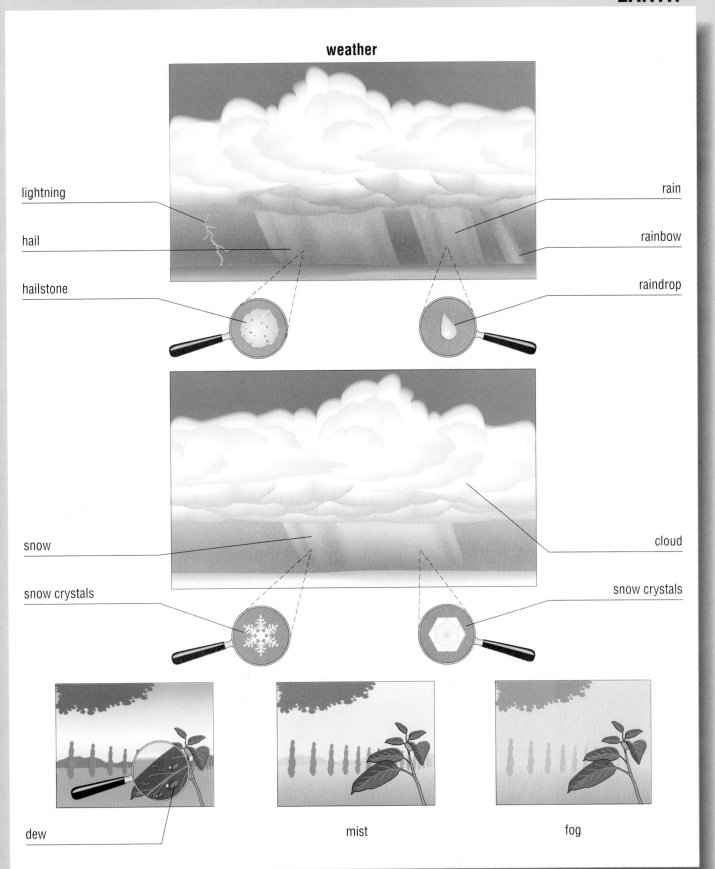

lightning

hail

hailstone

rain

rainbow

raindrop

snow

cloud

snow crystals

snow crystals

dew

mist

fog

VEGETAL KINGDOM

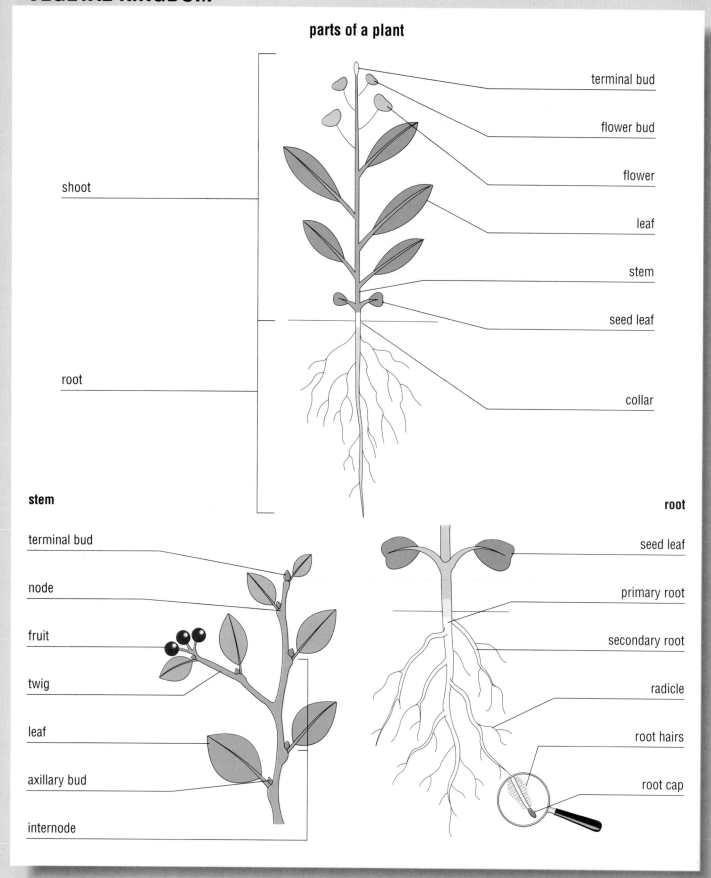

parts of a plant

terminal bud

flower bud

flower

leaf

stem

seed leaf

collar

shoot

root

stem

terminal bud

node

fruit

twig

leaf

axillary bud

internode

root

seed leaf

primary root

secondary root

radicle

root hairs

root cap

parts of a leaf

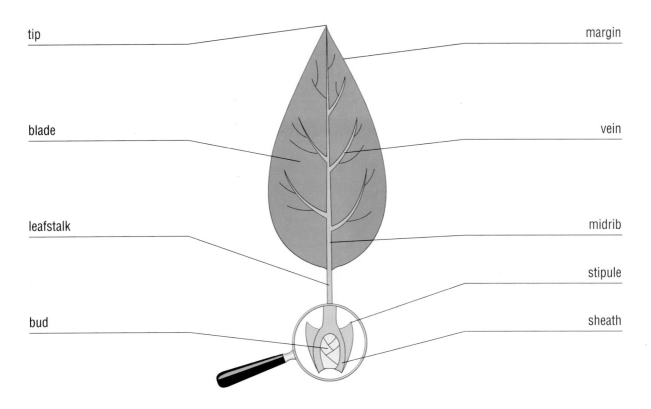

tip

margin

blade

vein

leafstalk

midrib

stipule

bud

sheath

parts of a flower

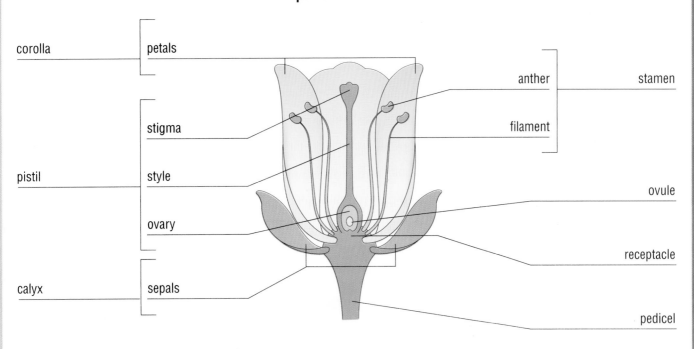

corolla

petals

anther

stamen

filament

stigma

pistil

style

ovule

ovary

receptacle

calyx

sepals

pedicel

VEGETAL KINGDOM

parts of a tree

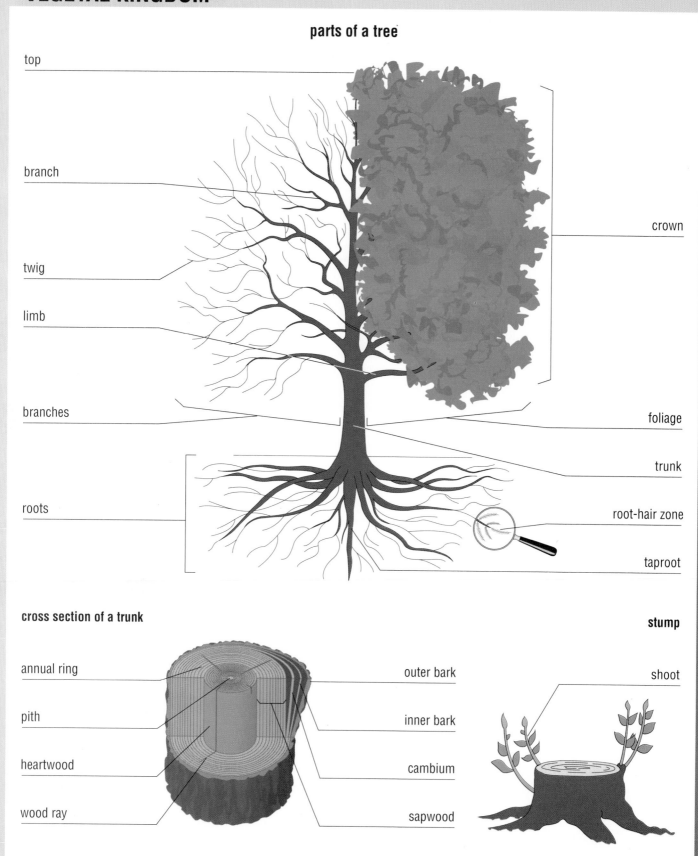

top

branch

twig

limb

branches

roots

crown

foliage

trunk

root-hair zone

taproot

cross section of a trunk

annual ring

pith

heartwood

wood ray

outer bark

inner bark

cambium

sapwood

stump

shoot

parts of a mushroom

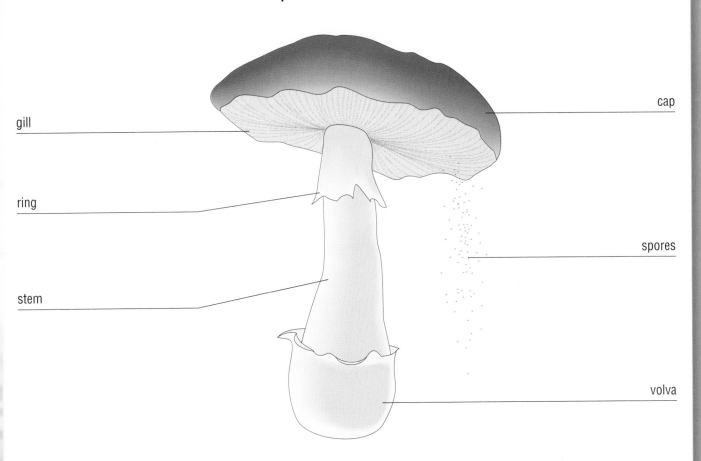

cap

gill

ring

spores

stem

volva

edible mushroom

morel

poisonous mushroom

fly agaric

deadly poisonous mushroom

destroying angel

horse

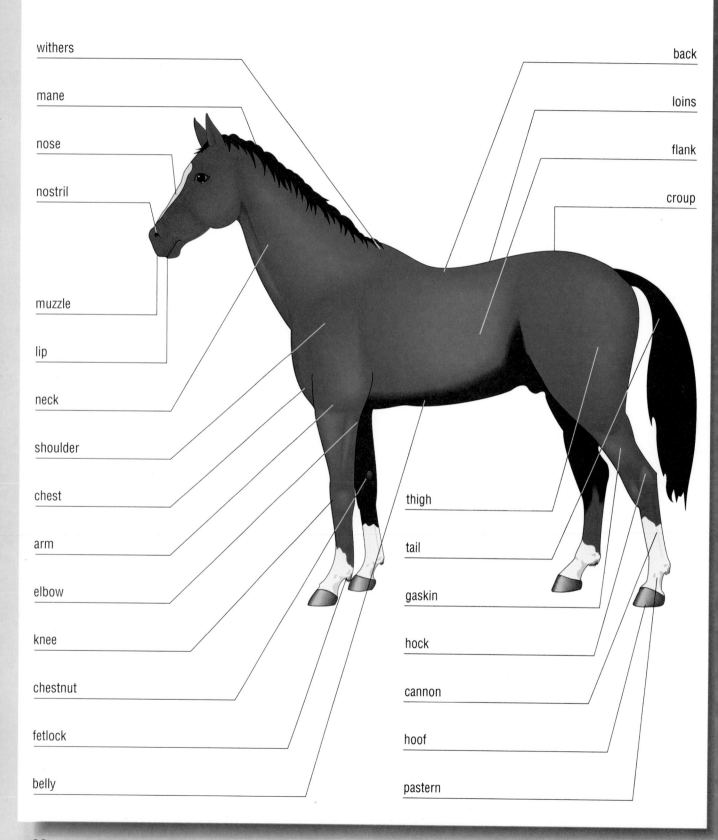

withers

mane

nose

nostril

muzzle

lip

neck

shoulder

chest

arm

elbow

knee

chestnut

fetlock

belly

thigh

tail

gaskin

hock

cannon

hoof

pastern

back

loins

flank

croup

dog

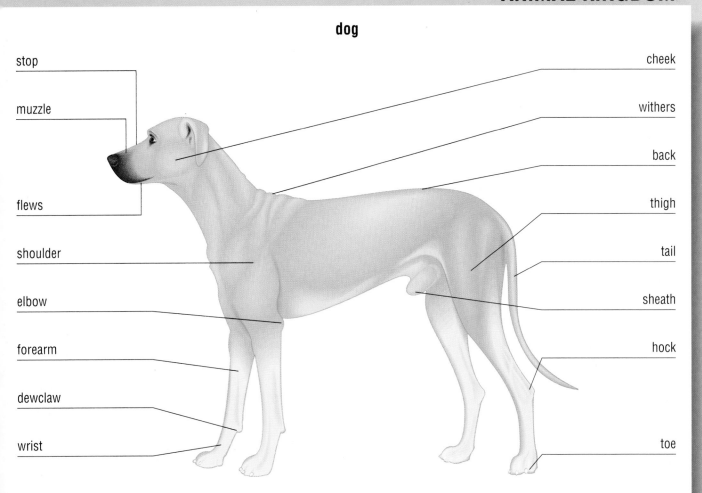

stop

muzzle

flews

shoulder

elbow

forearm

dewclaw

wrist

cheek

withers

back

thigh

tail

sheath

hock

toe

cat

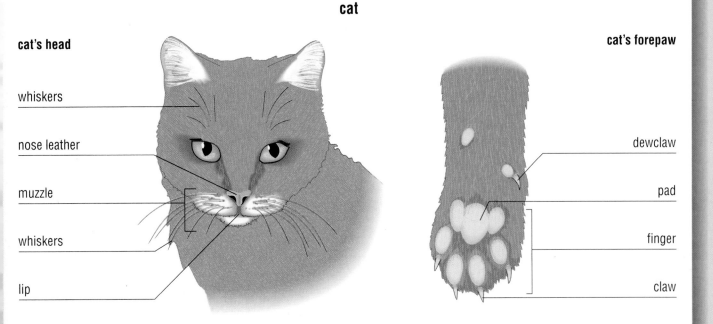

cat's head

whiskers

nose leather

muzzle

whiskers

lip

cat's forepaw

dewclaw

pad

finger

claw

bird

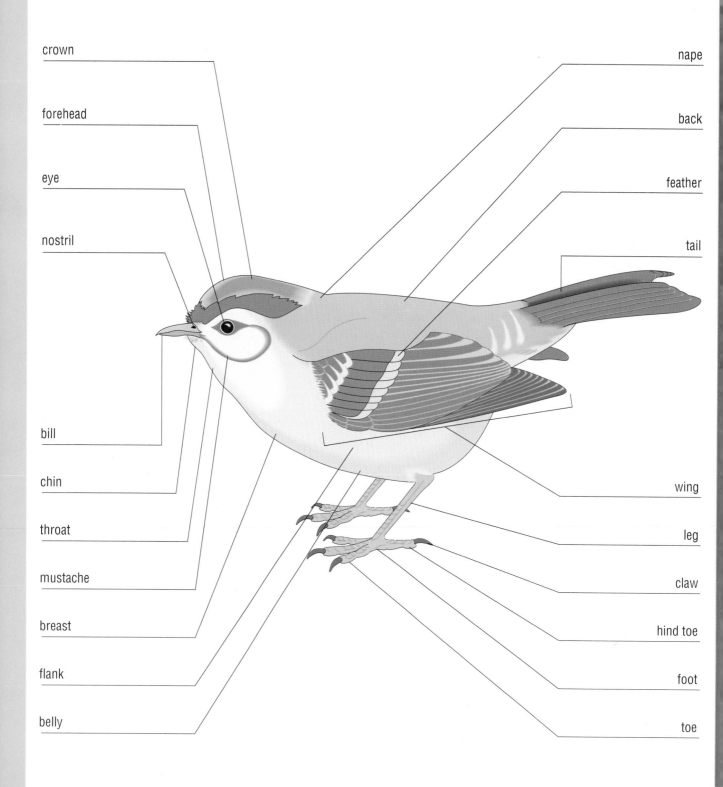

crown

forehead

eye

nostril

bill

chin

throat

mustache

breast

flank

belly

nape

back

feather

tail

wing

leg

claw

hind toe

foot

toe

major types of bills

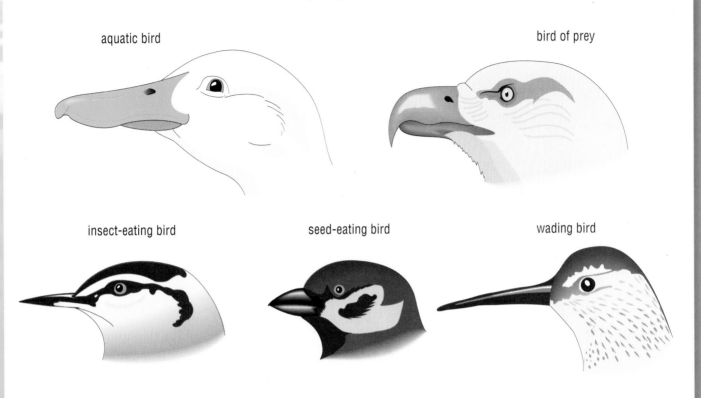

aquatic bird

bird of prey

insect-eating bird

seed-eating bird

wading bird

major types of feet

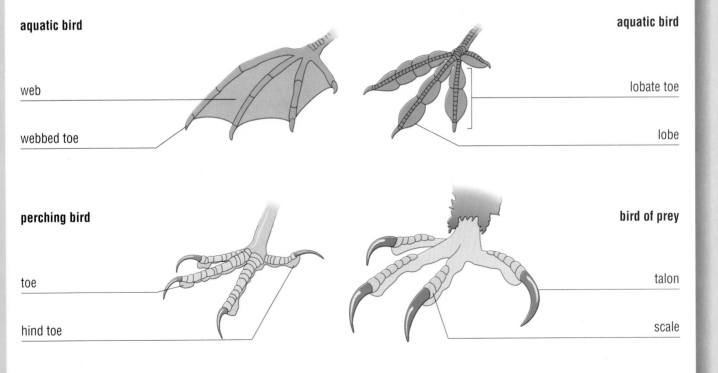

aquatic bird

web

webbed toe

aquatic bird

lobate toe

lobe

perching bird

toe

hind toe

bird of prey

talon

scale

butterfly

caterpillar

head

simple eye

mandible

legs

prolegs

thorax

abdominal segment

chrysalis

spiracle

abdomen

wing

thorax

antenna

butterfly

antenna

head

labial palp

compound eye

proboscis

foreleg

middle leg

forewing

wing vein

hind wing

thorax

abdomen

spiracle

hind leg

claw

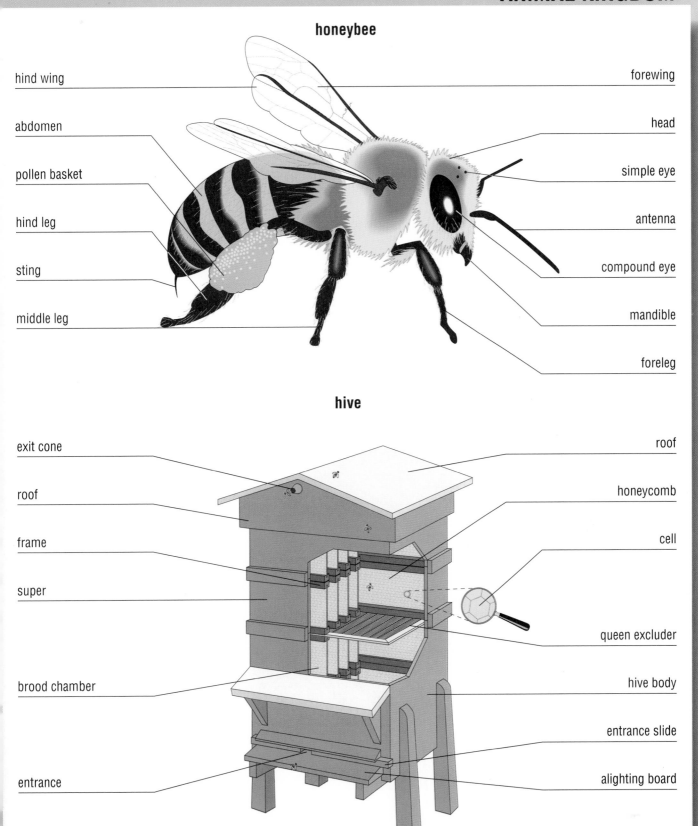

honeybee

hind wing

abdomen

pollen basket

hind leg

sting

middle leg

forewing

head

simple eye

antenna

compound eye

mandible

foreleg

hive

exit cone

roof

frame

super

brood chamber

entrance

roof

honeycomb

cell

queen excluder

hive body

entrance slide

alighting board

gastropod: snail

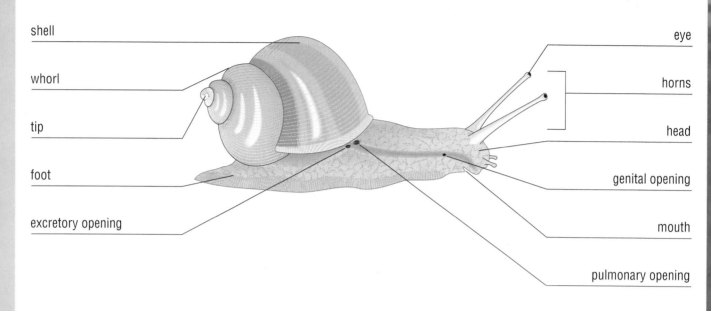

shell

whorl

tip

foot

excretory opening

eye

horns

head

genital opening

mouth

pulmonary opening

crustacean: lobster

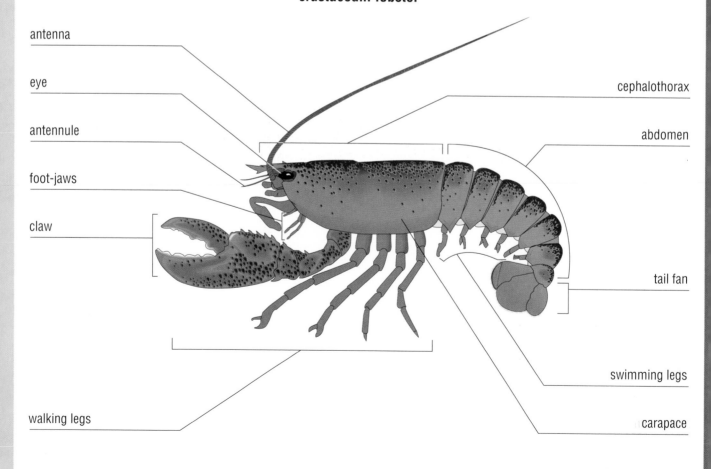

antenna

eye

antennule

foot-jaws

claw

cephalothorax

abdomen

tail fan

swimming legs

walking legs

carapace

batrachian: frog

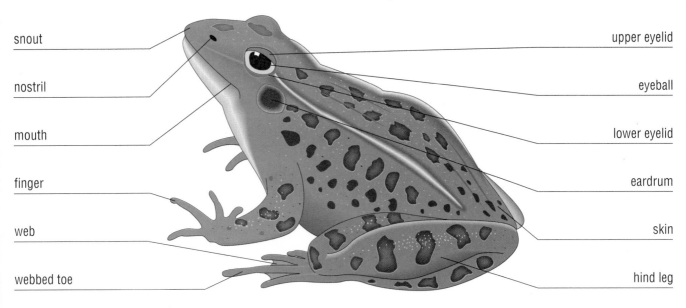

snout

nostril

mouth

finger

web

webbed toe

upper eyelid

eyeball

lower eyelid

eardrum

skin

hind leg

fish

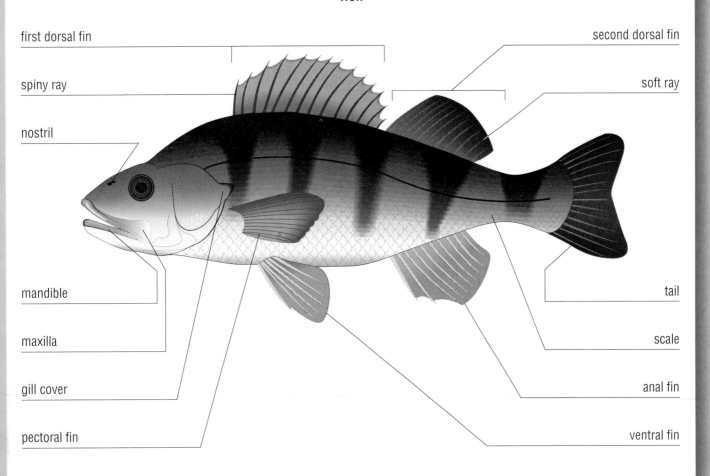

first dorsal fin

spiny ray

nostril

mandible

maxilla

gill cover

pectoral fin

second dorsal fin

soft ray

tail

scale

anal fin

ventral fin

turtle

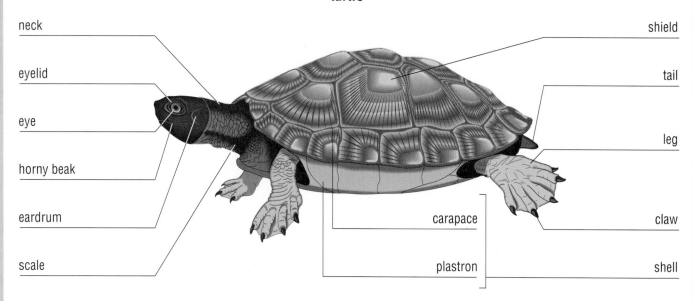

neck

eyelid

eye

horny beak

eardrum

scale

shield

tail

leg

claw

shell

carapace

plastron

venomous snake

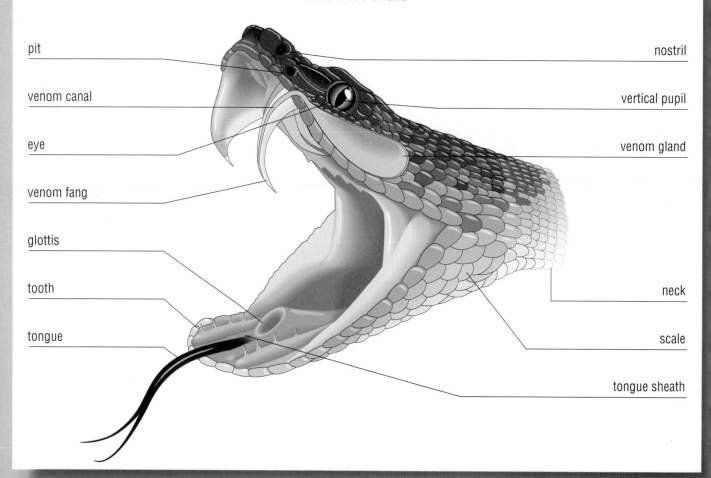

pit

venom canal

eye

venom fang

glottis

tooth

tongue

nostril

vertical pupil

venom gland

neck

scale

tongue sheath

wild animals

lion

rhinoceros

zebra

crocodile

elephant

giraffe

ANIMAL KINGDOM

wild animals

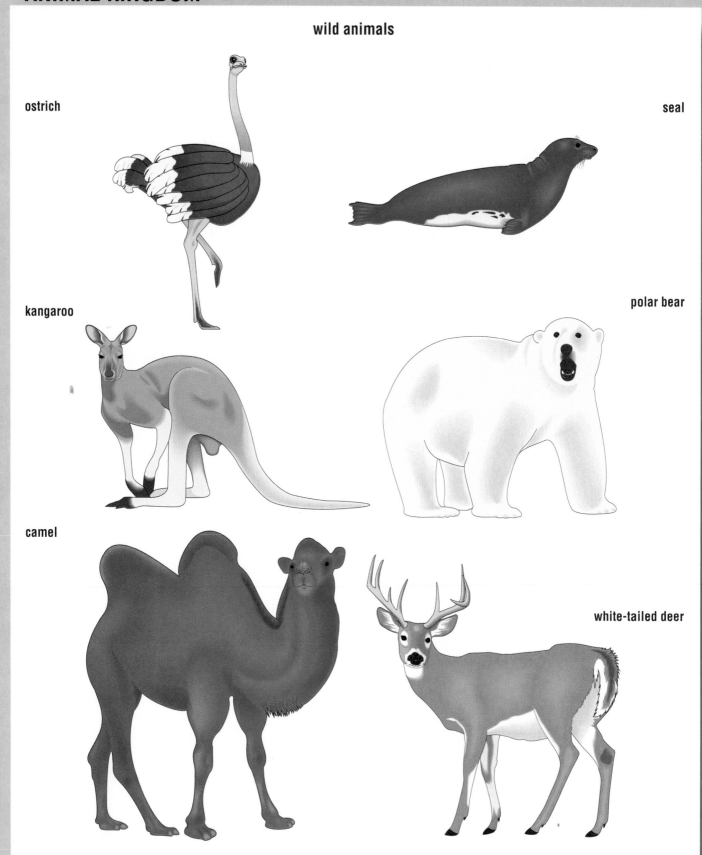

ostrich

seal

kangaroo

polar bear

camel

white-tailed deer

body, front view

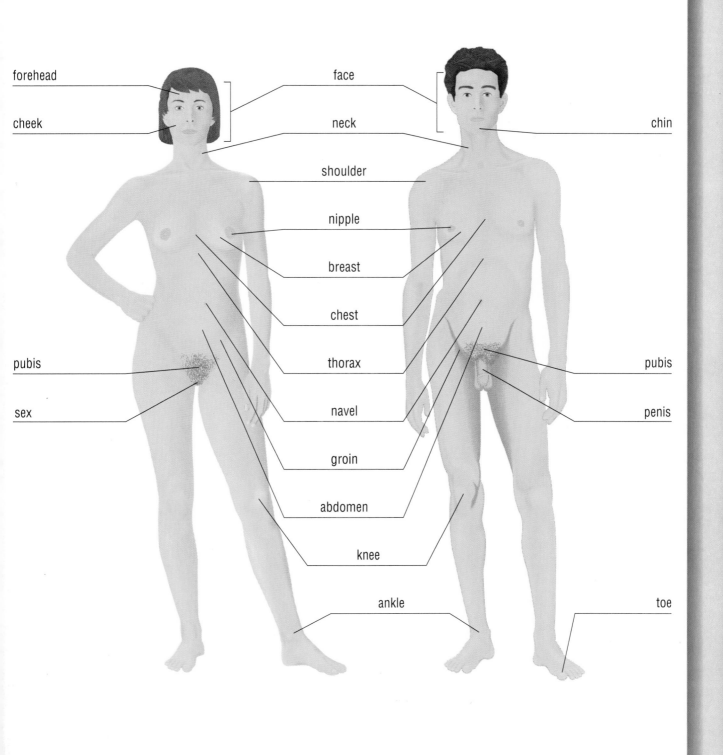

forehead

cheek

face

neck

chin

shoulder

nipple

breast

chest

thorax

pubis

navel

pubis

sex

groin

penis

abdomen

knee

ankle

toe

HUMAN BODY

body, rear view

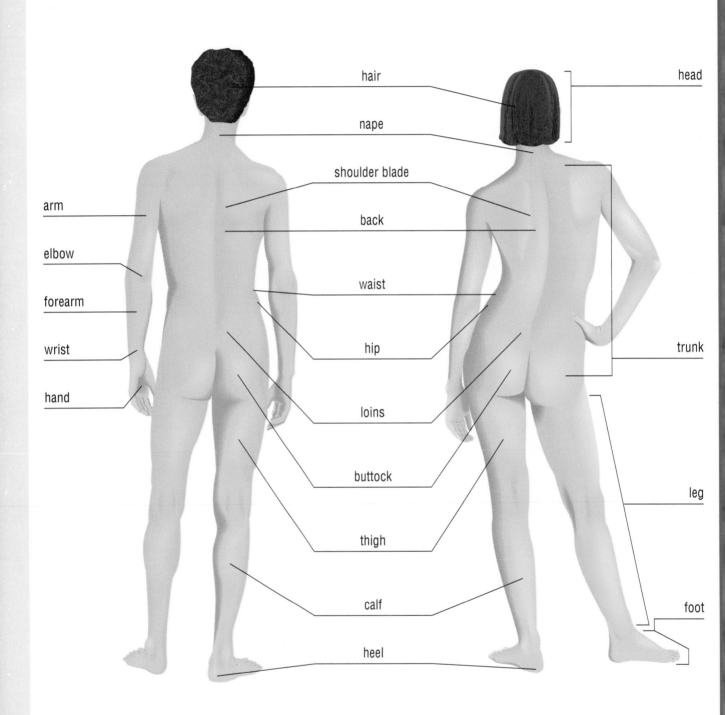

hair

nape

head

shoulder blade

back

arm

elbow

forearm

waist

wrist

trunk

hand

hip

loins

buttock

leg

thigh

calf

foot

heel

skeleton

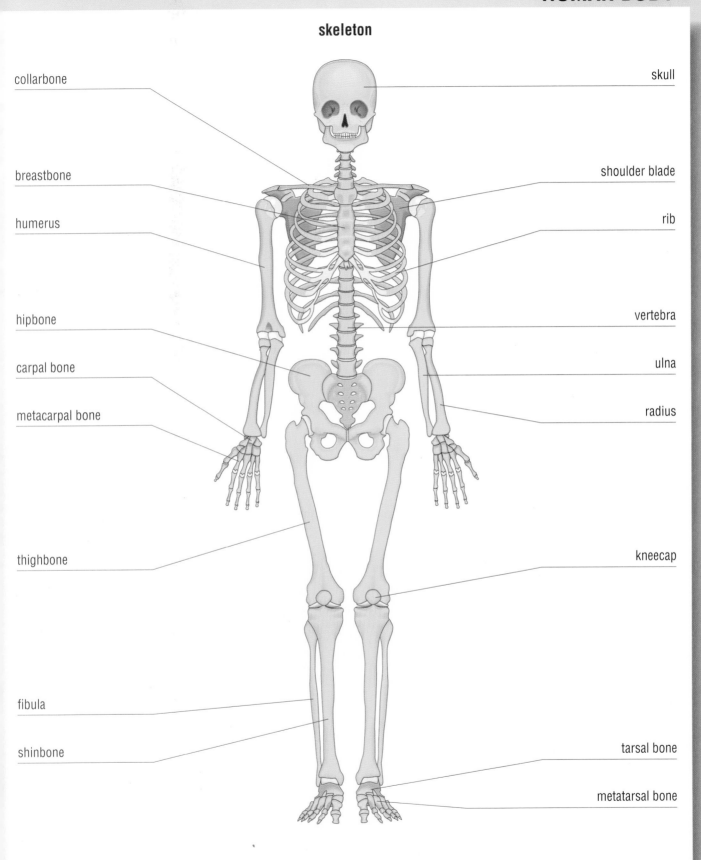

collarbone

breastbone

humerus

hipbone

carpal bone

metacarpal bone

thighbone

fibula

shinbone

skull

shoulder blade

rib

vertebra

ulna

radius

kneecap

tarsal bone

metatarsal bone

human denture

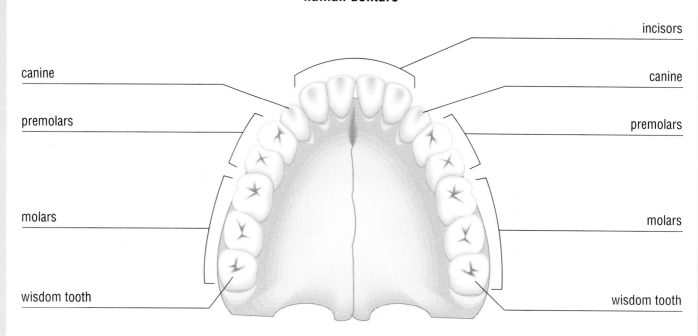

incisors

canine

canine

premolars

premolars

molars

molars

wisdom tooth

wisdom tooth

mouth: the organ of taste

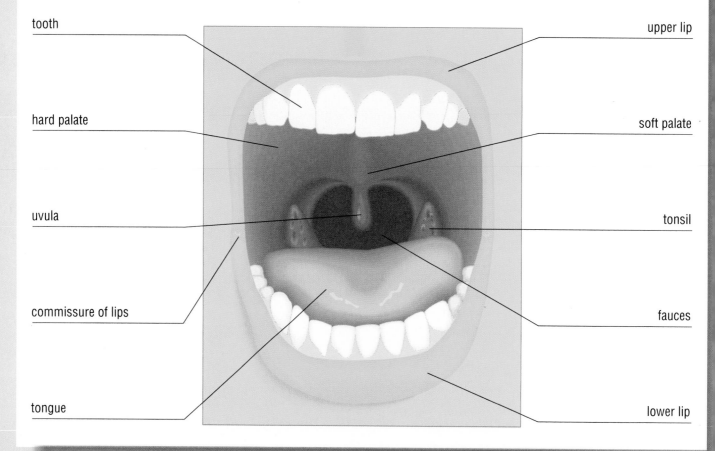

tooth

upper lip

hard palate

soft palate

uvula

tonsil

commissure of lips

fauces

tongue

lower lip

eye: the organ of sight

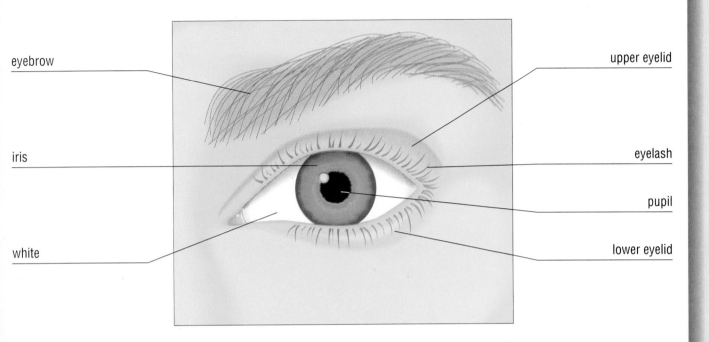

eyebrow

upper eyelid

iris

eyelash

pupil

white

lower eyelid

ear: the organ of hearing

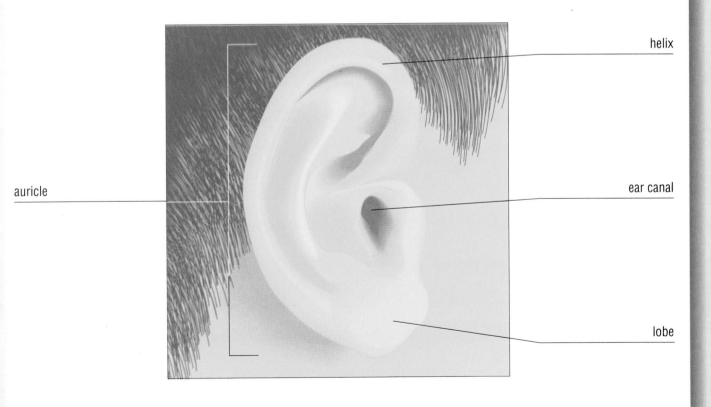

helix

auricle

ear canal

lobe

nose: the organ of smell

root of nose

dorsum

nostril

ala

philtrum

tip of nose

hand: the organ of touch

thumb

lunule

index finger

fingernail

middle finger

palm

third finger

little finger

wrist

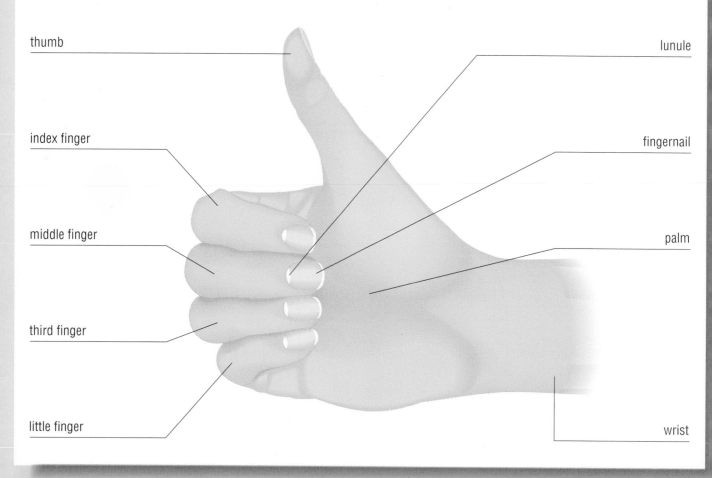

bread

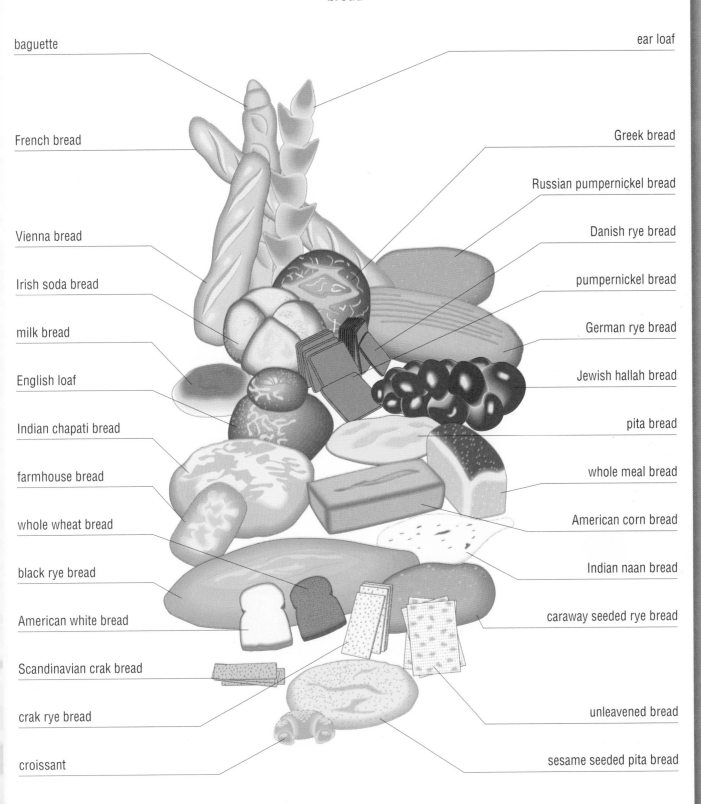

baguette

ear loaf

French bread

Greek bread

Russian pumpernickel bread

Vienna bread

Danish rye bread

Irish soda bread

pumpernickel bread

milk bread

German rye bread

English loaf

Jewish hallah bread

Indian chapati bread

pita bread

farmhouse bread

whole meal bread

whole wheat bread

American corn bread

black rye bread

Indian naan bread

American white bread

caraway seeded rye bread

Scandinavian crak bread

crak rye bread

unleavened bread

croissant

sesame seeded pita bread

leaf vegetables

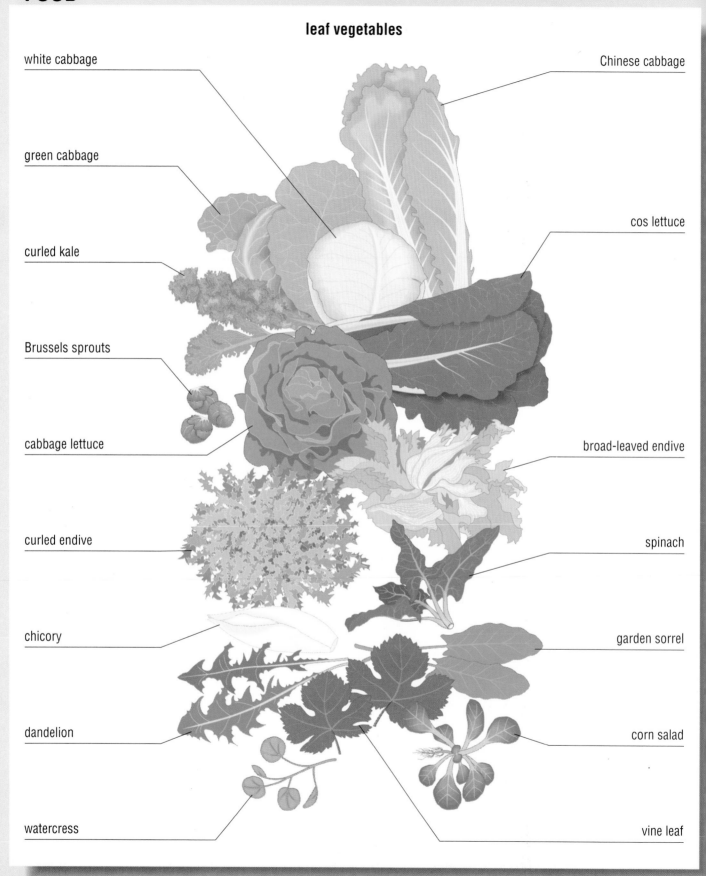

white cabbage

Chinese cabbage

green cabbage

cos lettuce

curled kale

Brussels sprouts

cabbage lettuce

broad-leaved endive

curled endive

spinach

chicory

garden sorrel

dandelion

corn salad

watercress

vine leaf

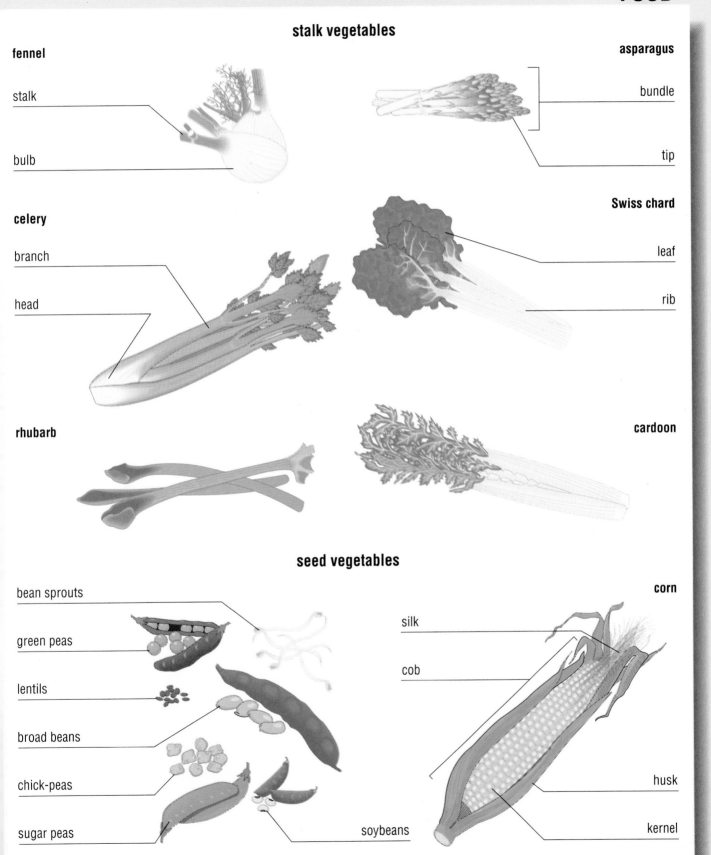

stalk vegetables

fennel

stalk

bulb

asparagus

bundle

tip

celery

branch

head

Swiss chard

leaf

rib

rhubarb

cardoon

seed vegetables

bean sprouts

green peas

lentils

broad beans

chick-peas

sugar peas

soybeans

corn

silk

cob

husk

kernel

tuber vegetables

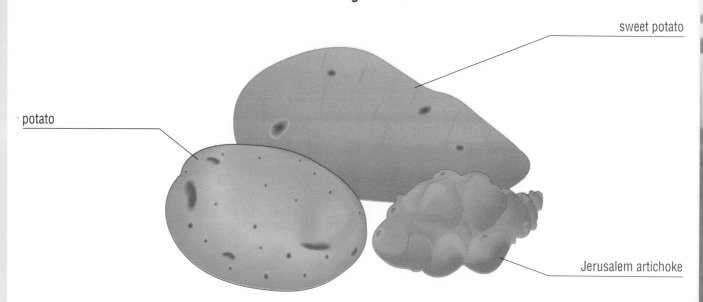

sweet potato

potato

Jerusalem artichoke

root vegetables

kohlrabi

celeriac

horseradish

parsnip

black salsify

carrot

turnip

beet

rutabaga

radish

salsify

inflorescent vegetables

cauliflower

broccoli

artichoke

bulb vegetables

Spanish onion

leek

pickling onion

scallion

garlic

shallot

chive

fruit vegetables

autumn squash

watermelon

muskmelon

cantaloupe

pumpkin

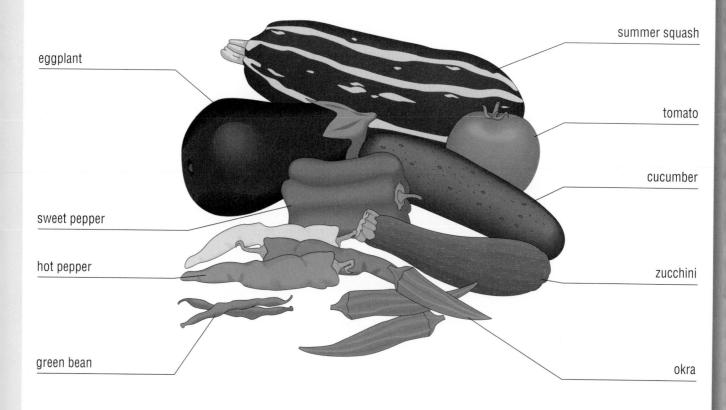

summer squash

eggplant

tomato

cucumber

sweet pepper

hot pepper

zucchini

green bean

okra

pome fruits

apple

pear

quince

Japanese plum

stone fruits

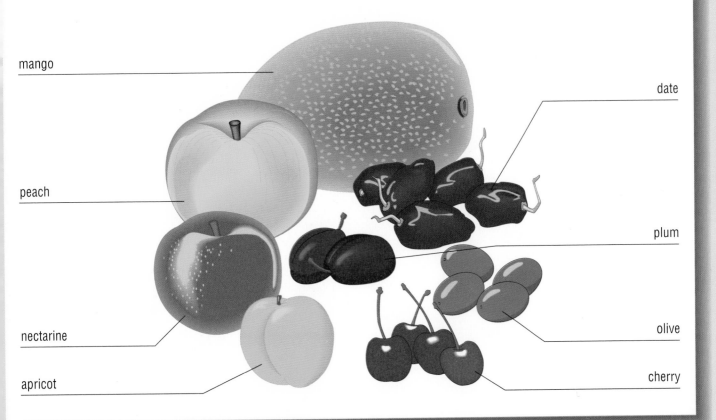

mango

date

peach

plum

nectarine

olive

apricot

cherry

FOOD

berries

cranberry

currant

gooseberry

huckleberry

grape

black currant

blueberry

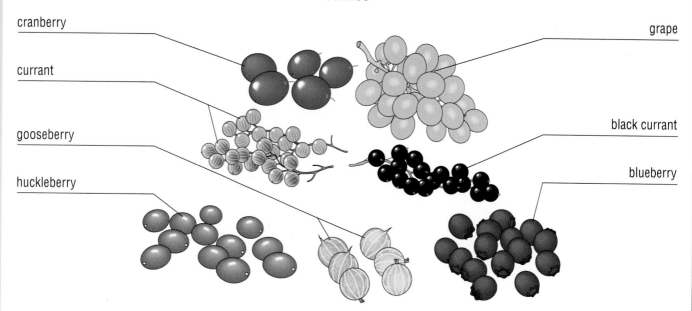

citrus fruits

grapefruit

orange

mandarin

kumquat

lemon

tropical fruits

pineapple

banana

pomegranate

papaya

avocado

cherimoya

kiwi

guava

Japanese persimmon

litchi

Indian fig

nuts

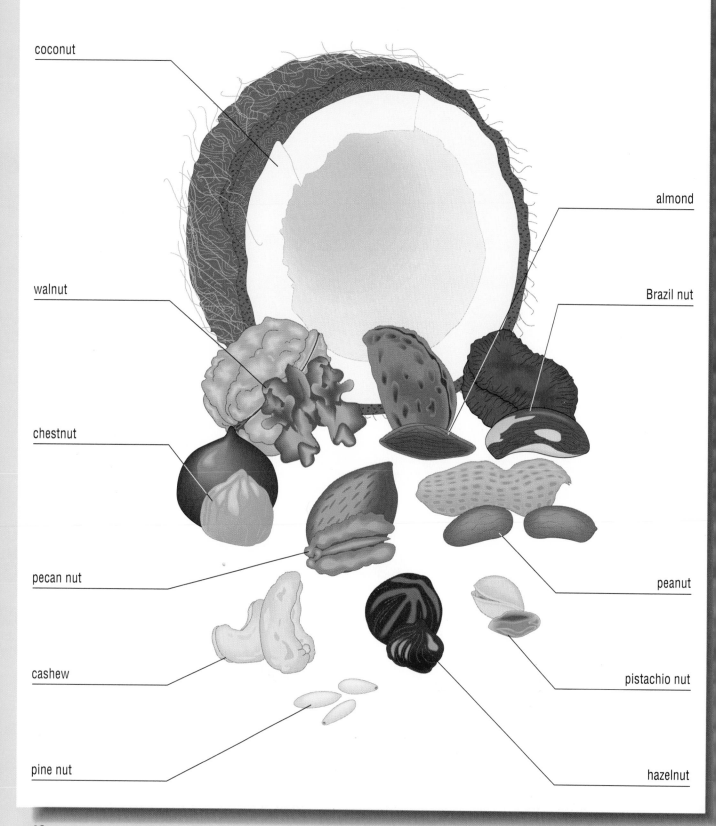

coconut

almond

walnut

Brazil nut

chestnut

pecan nut

peanut

cashew

pistachio nut

pine nut

hazelnut

cheeses

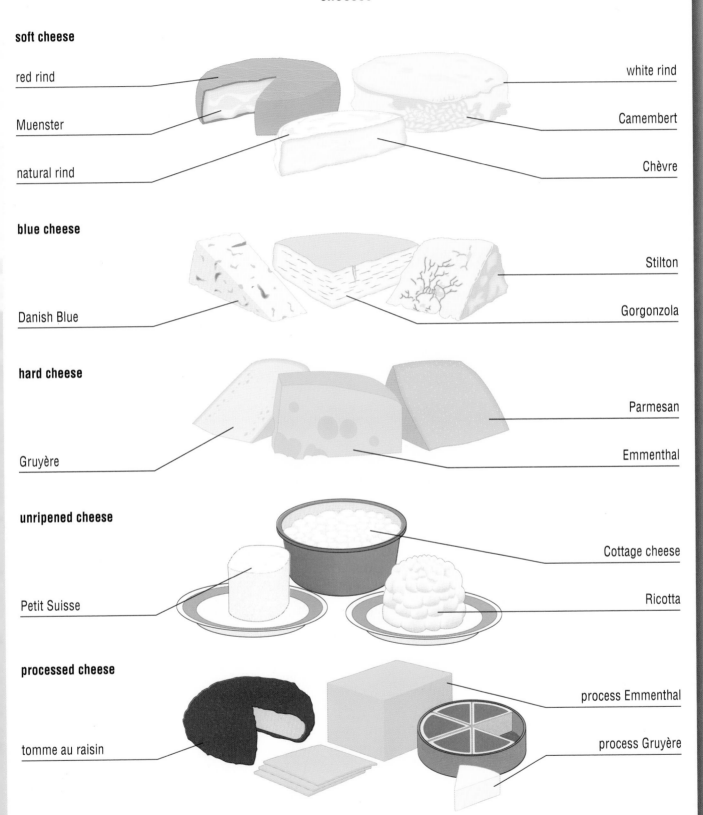

soft cheese

red rind

Muenster

natural rind

white rind

Camembert

Chèvre

blue cheese

Danish Blue

Stilton

Gorgonzola

hard cheese

Gruyère

Parmesan

Emmenthal

unripened cheese

Petit Suisse

Cottage cheese

Ricotta

processed cheese

tomme au raisin

process Emmenthal

process Gruyère

FOOD

desserts

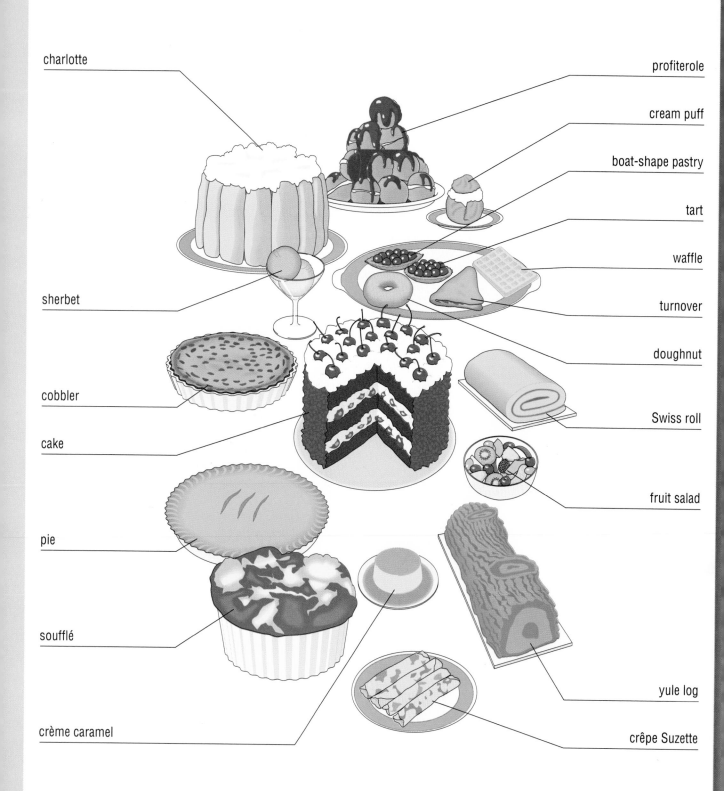

charlotte

profiterole

cream puff

boat-shape pastry

tart

waffle

sherbet

turnover

doughnut

cobbler

cake

Swiss roll

fruit salad

pie

soufflé

yule log

crème caramel

crêpe Suzette

farmstead

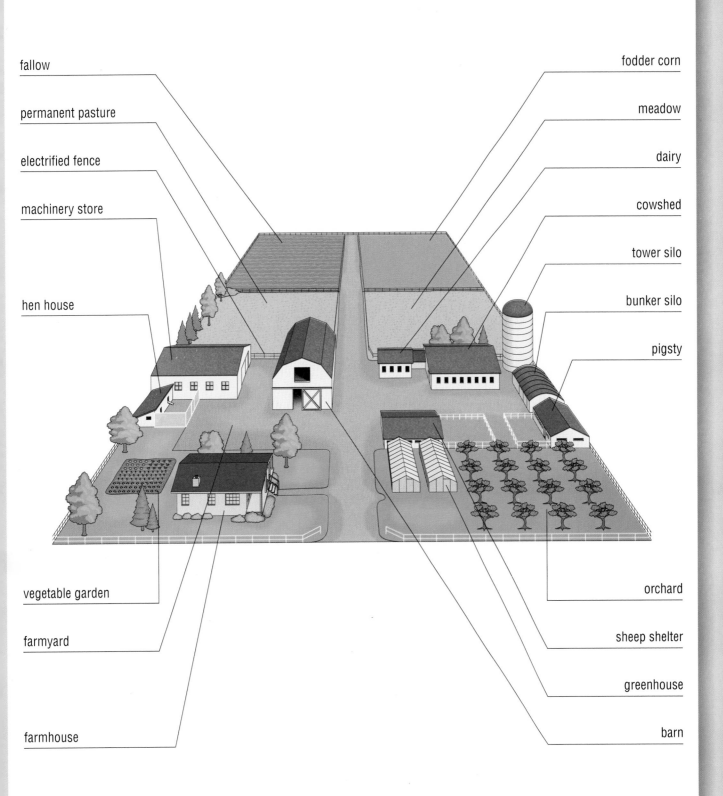

fallow

permanent pasture

electrified fence

machinery store

hen house

vegetable garden

farmyard

farmhouse

fodder corn

meadow

dairy

cowshed

tower silo

bunker silo

pigsty

orchard

sheep shelter

greenhouse

barn

FARMING

farm's animals

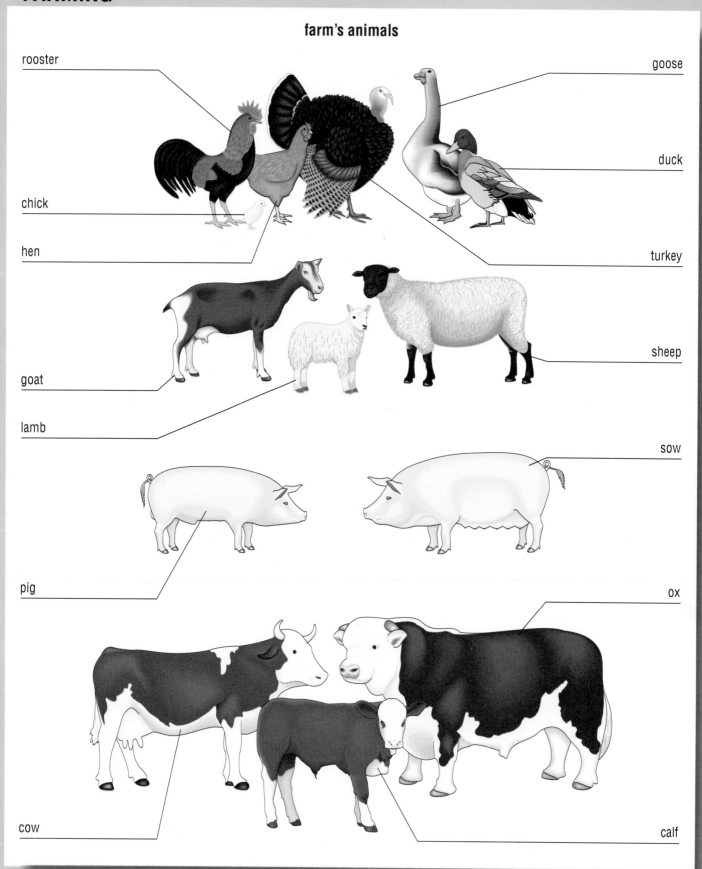

rooster

chick

hen

goat

lamb

pig

cow

goose

duck

turkey

sheep

sow

ox

calf

pleasure garden

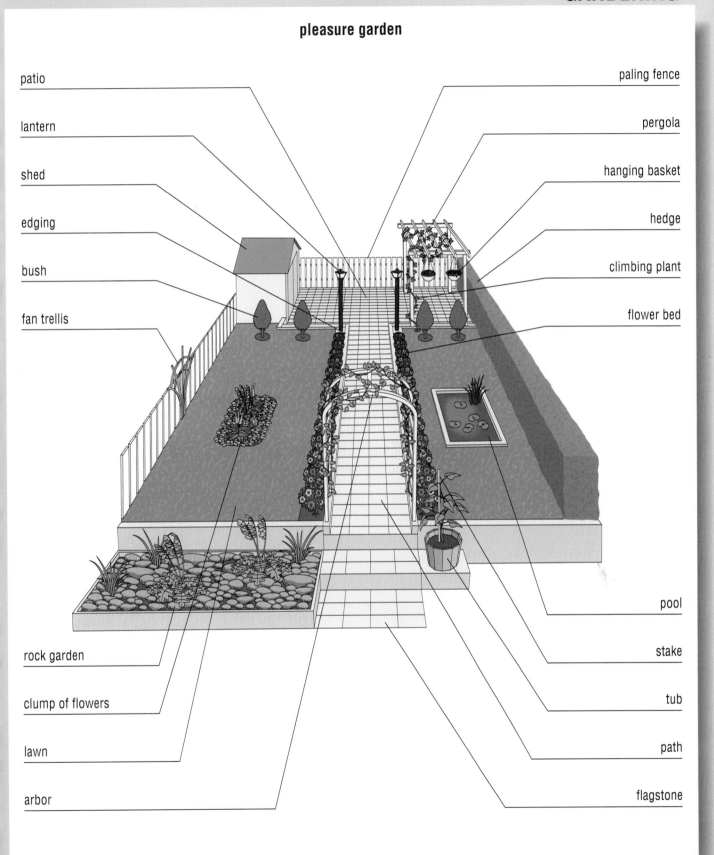

patio

lantern

shed

edging

bush

fan trellis

paling fence

pergola

hanging basket

hedge

climbing plant

flower bed

rock garden

clump of flowers

lawn

arbor

pool

stake

tub

path

flagstone

GARDENING

tools and equipment

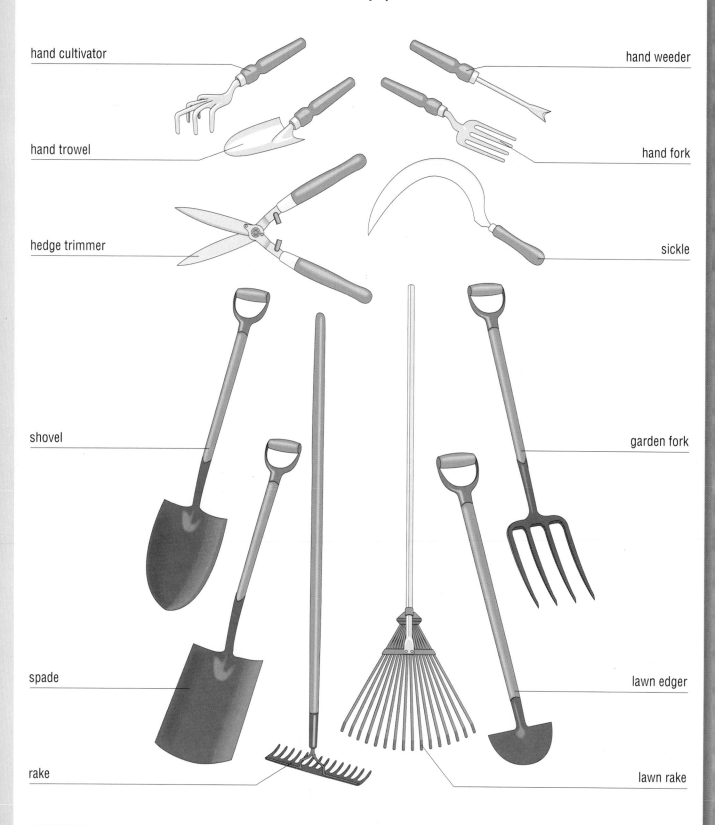

hand cultivator

hand weeder

hand trowel

hand fork

hedge trimmer

sickle

shovel

garden fork

spade

lawn edger

rake

lawn rake

tools and equipment

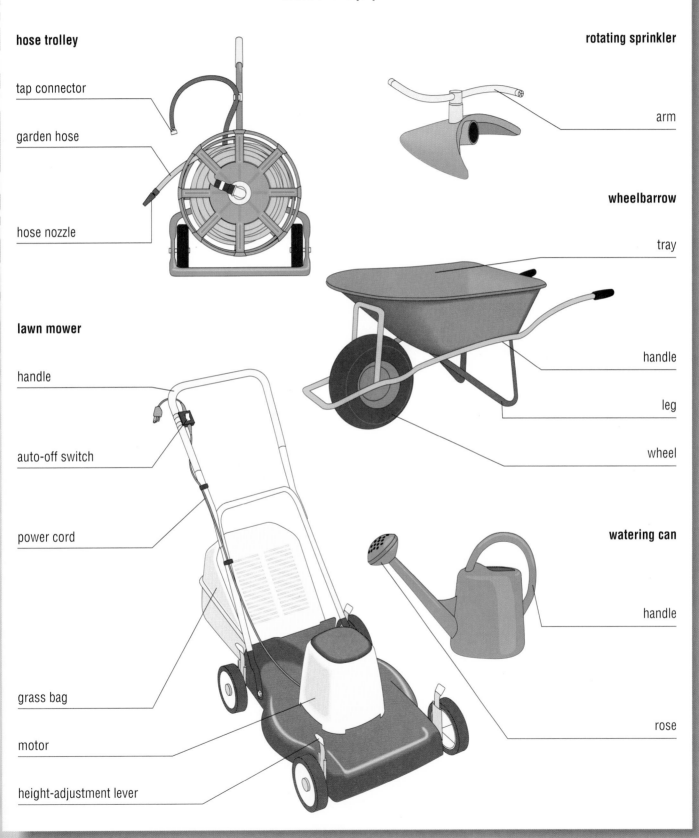

hose trolley

tap connector

garden hose

hose nozzle

lawn mower

handle

auto-off switch

power cord

grass bag

motor

height-adjustment lever

rotating sprinkler

arm

wheelbarrow

tray

handle

leg

wheel

watering can

handle

rose

ARCHITECTURE

traditional houses

yurt
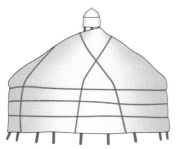

hut

igloo

isba

wigwam

hut

tepee

pile dwelling

castle

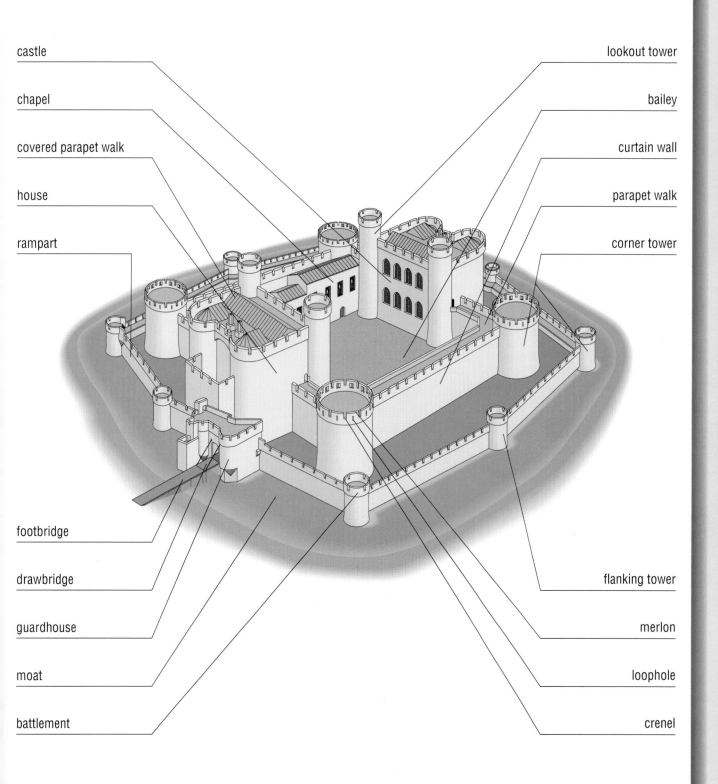

castle

chapel

covered parapet walk

house

rampart

footbridge

drawbridge

guardhouse

moat

battlement

lookout tower

bailey

curtain wall

parapet walk

corner tower

flanking tower

merlon

loophole

crenel

HOUSE

exterior of a house

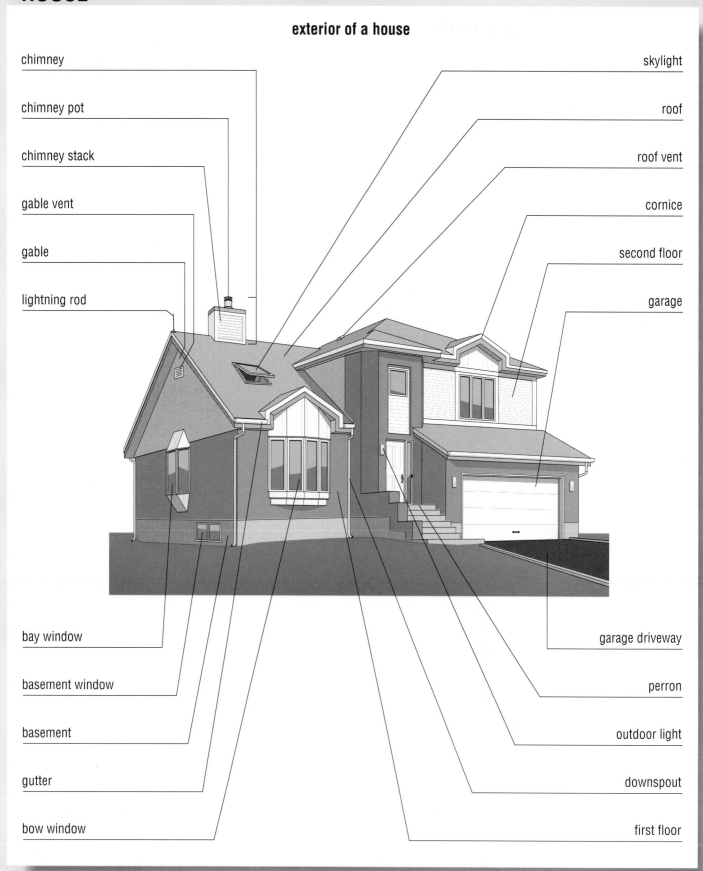

chimney

chimney pot

chimney stack

gable vent

gable

lightning rod

skylight

roof

roof vent

cornice

second floor

garage

bay window

basement window

basement

gutter

bow window

garage driveway

perron

outdoor light

downspout

first floor

exterior door

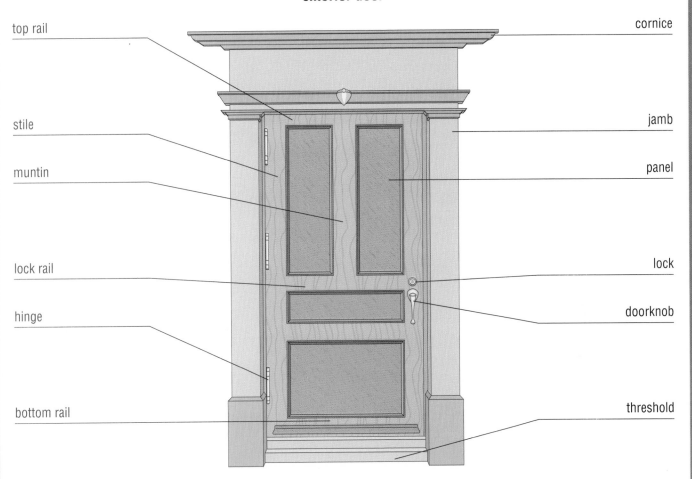

top rail

stile

muntin

lock rail

hinge

bottom rail

cornice

jamb

panel

lock

doorknob

threshold

window

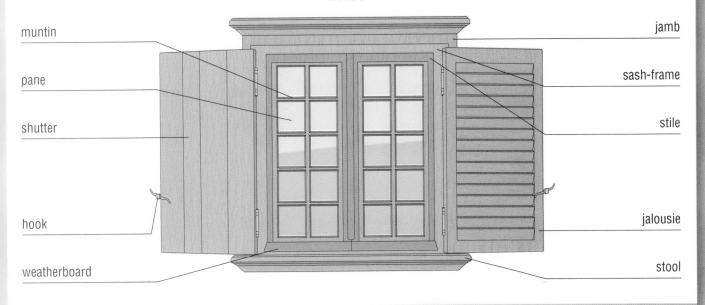

muntin

pane

shutter

hook

weatherboard

jamb

sash-frame

stile

jalousie

stool

stairs

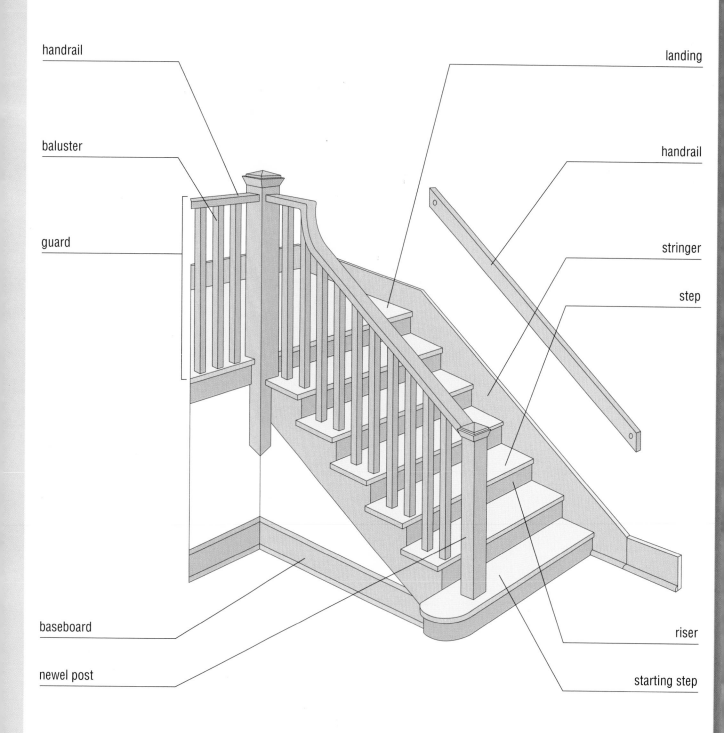

handrail

baluster

guard

landing

handrail

stringer

step

baseboard

newel post

riser

starting step

bathroom

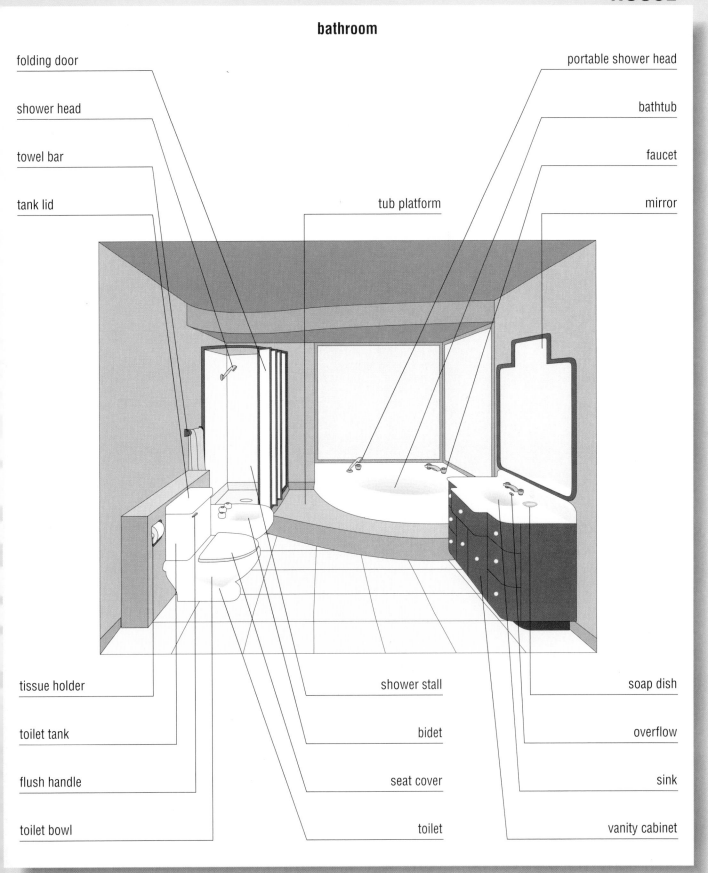

folding door

portable shower head

shower head

bathtub

towel bar

faucet

tank lid

tub platform

mirror

tissue holder

shower stall

soap dish

toilet tank

bidet

overflow

flush handle

seat cover

sink

toilet bowl

toilet

vanity cabinet

side chair

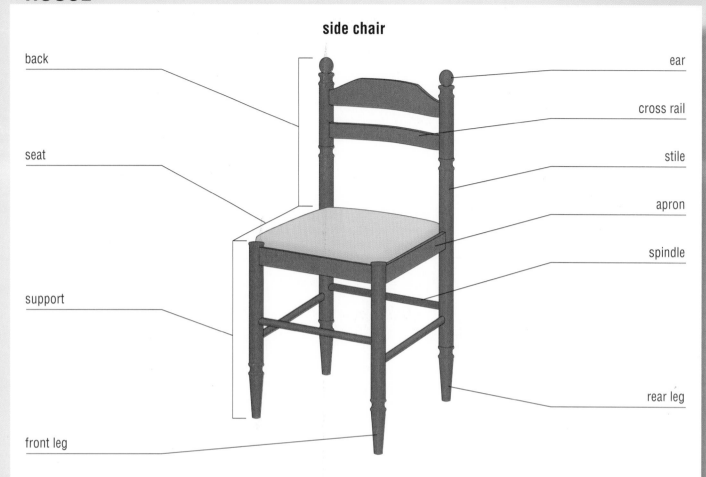

back

ear

cross rail

seat

stile

apron

spindle

support

rear leg

front leg

gate-leg table

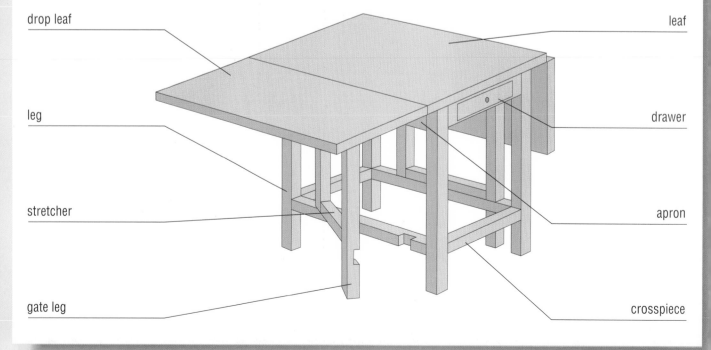

drop leaf

leaf

leg

drawer

stretcher

apron

gate leg

crosspiece

armchair

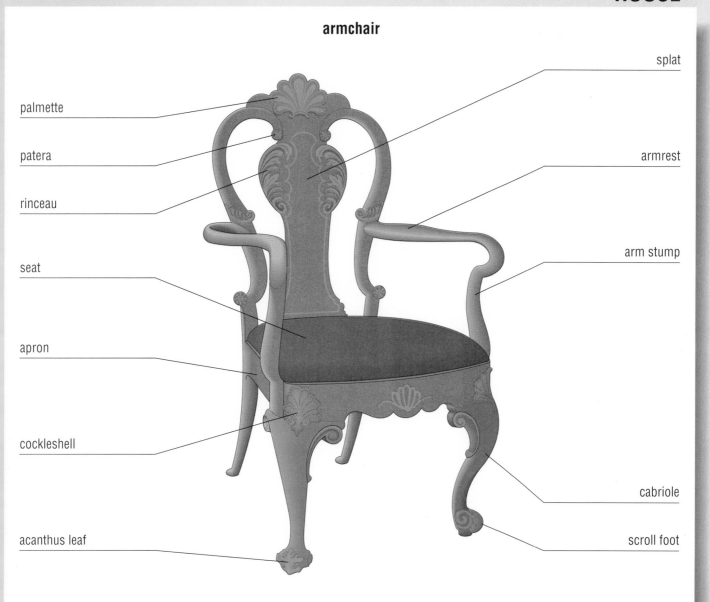

palmette

patera

rinceau

seat

apron

cockleshell

acanthus leaf

splat

armrest

arm stump

cabriole

scroll foot

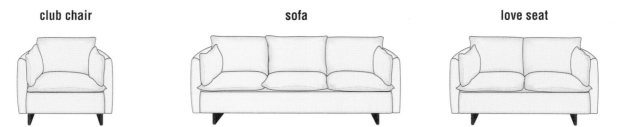

club chair

sofa

love seat

bed

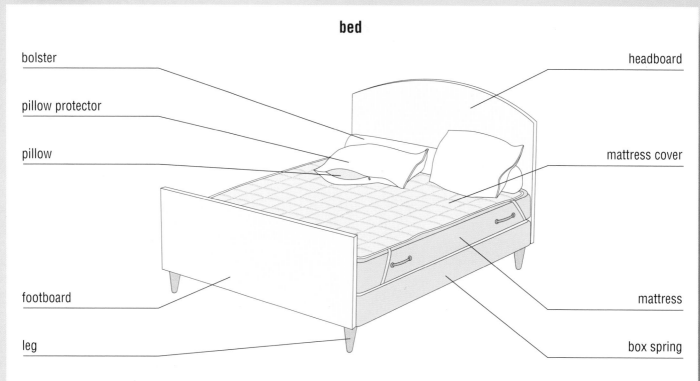

bolster

pillow protector

pillow

footboard

leg

headboard

mattress cover

mattress

box spring

linen

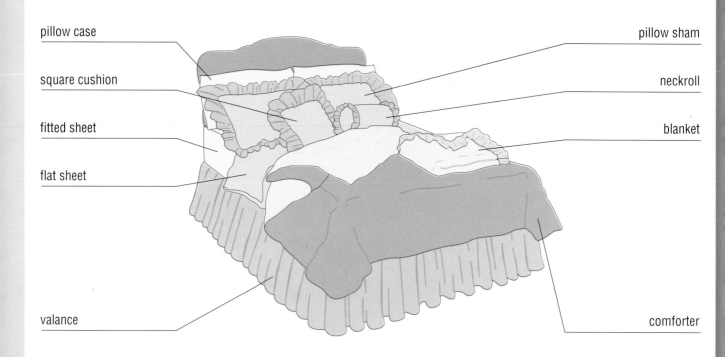

pillow case

square cushion

fitted sheet

flat sheet

valance

pillow sham

neckroll

blanket

comforter

lights

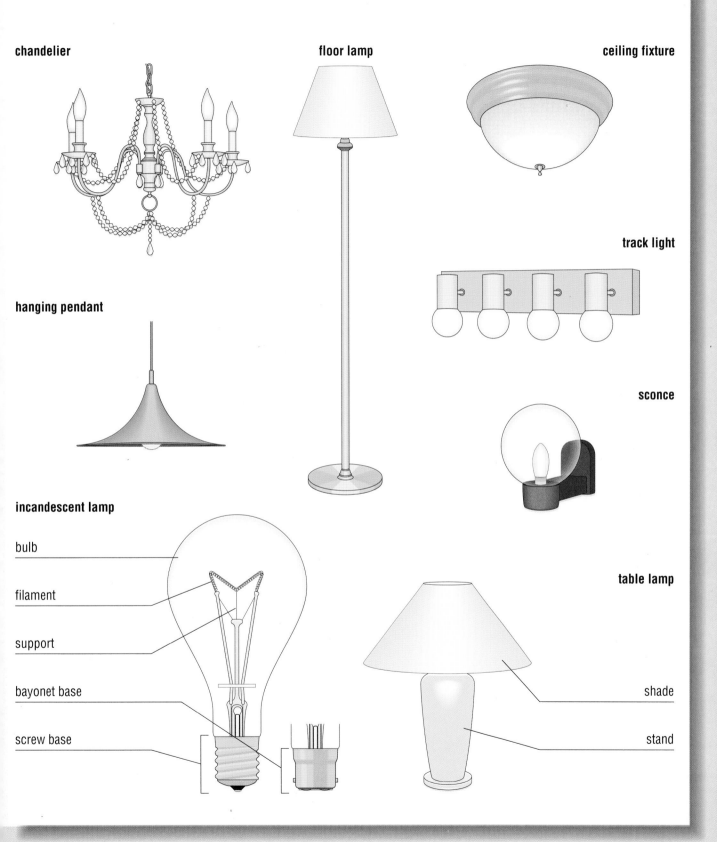

chandelier

floor lamp

ceiling fixture

track light

hanging pendant

sconce

incandescent lamp

bulb

filament

support

bayonet base

screw base

table lamp

shade

stand

dinnerware

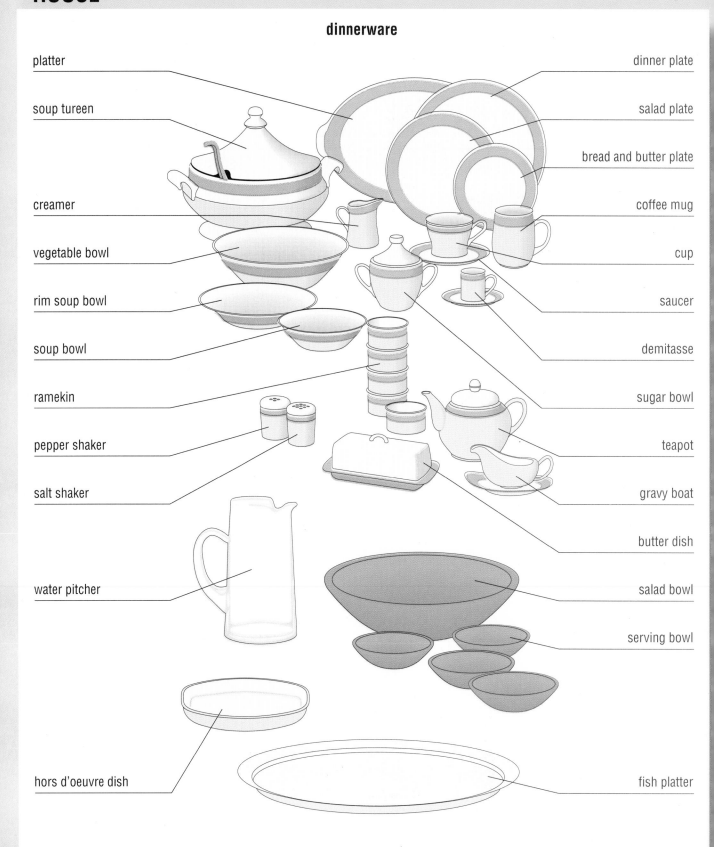

platter

soup tureen

creamer

vegetable bowl

rim soup bowl

soup bowl

ramekin

pepper shaker

salt shaker

water pitcher

hors d'oeuvre dish

dinner plate

salad plate

bread and butter plate

coffee mug

cup

saucer

demitasse

sugar bowl

teapot

gravy boat

butter dish

salad bowl

serving bowl

fish platter

silverware

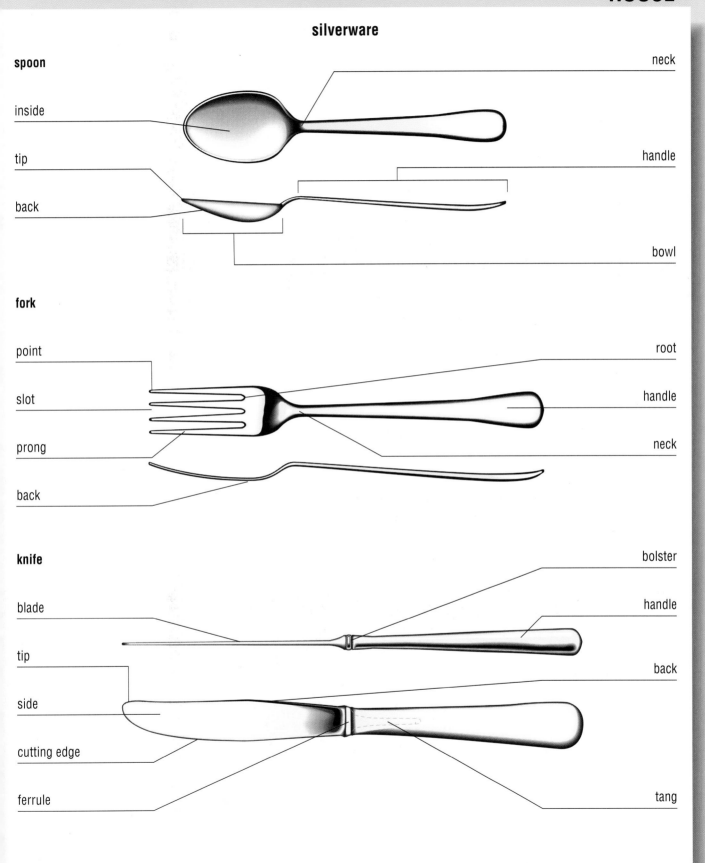

spoon

neck

inside

tip

handle

back

bowl

fork

point

root

slot

handle

prong

neck

back

knife

bolster

blade

handle

tip

back

side

cutting edge

ferrule

tang

kitchen utensils

set of utensils

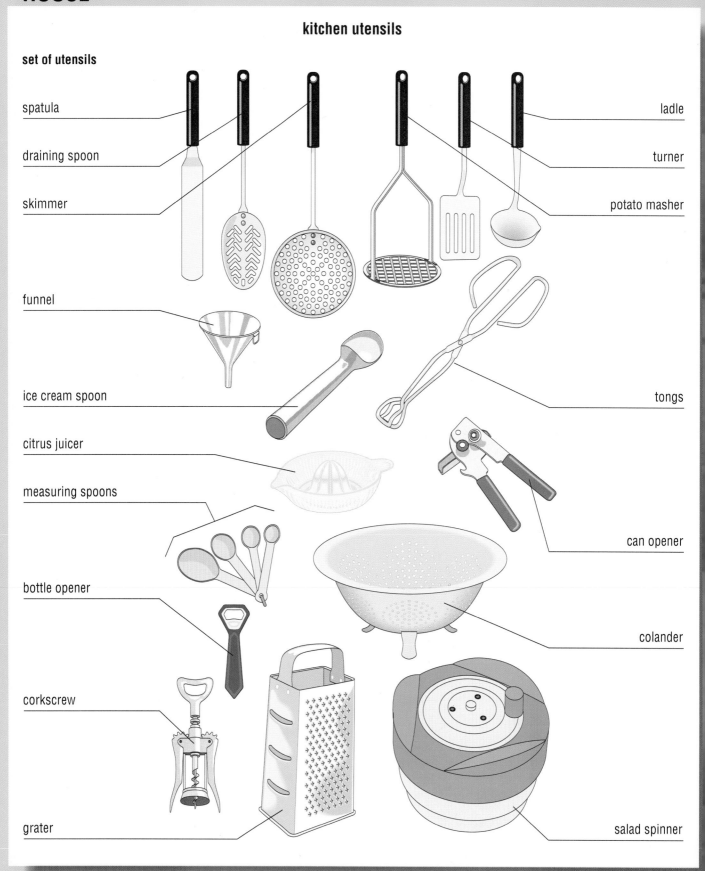

spatula

draining spoon

skimmer

funnel

ice cream spoon

citrus juicer

measuring spoons

bottle opener

corkscrew

grater

ladle

turner

potato masher

tongs

can opener

colander

salad spinner

cooking utensils

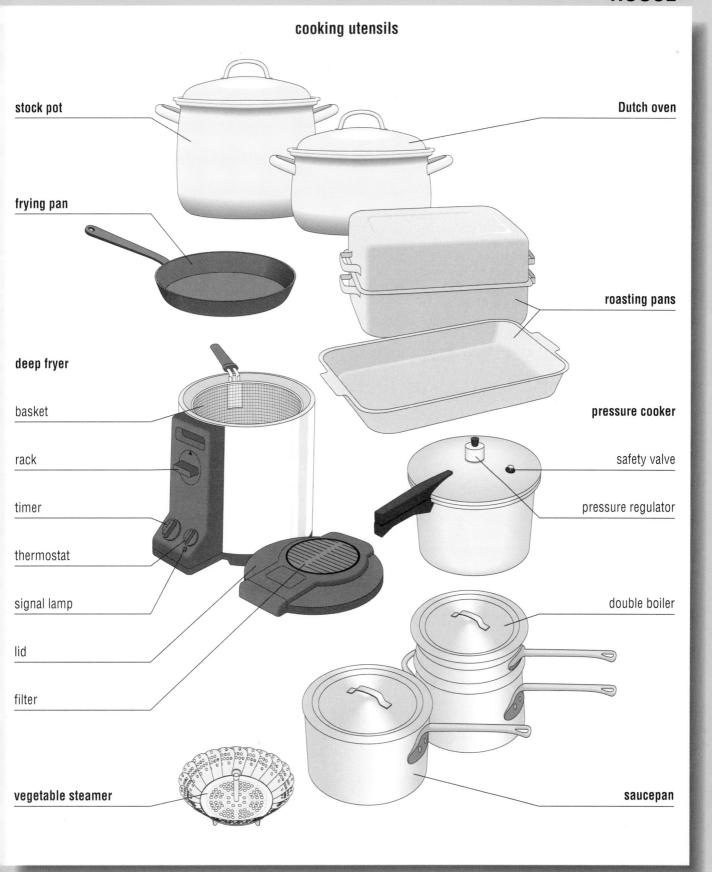

stock pot

Dutch oven

frying pan

roasting pans

deep fryer

basket

rack

timer

thermostat

signal lamp

lid

filter

pressure cooker

safety valve

pressure regulator

double boiler

saucepan

vegetable steamer

domestic appliances

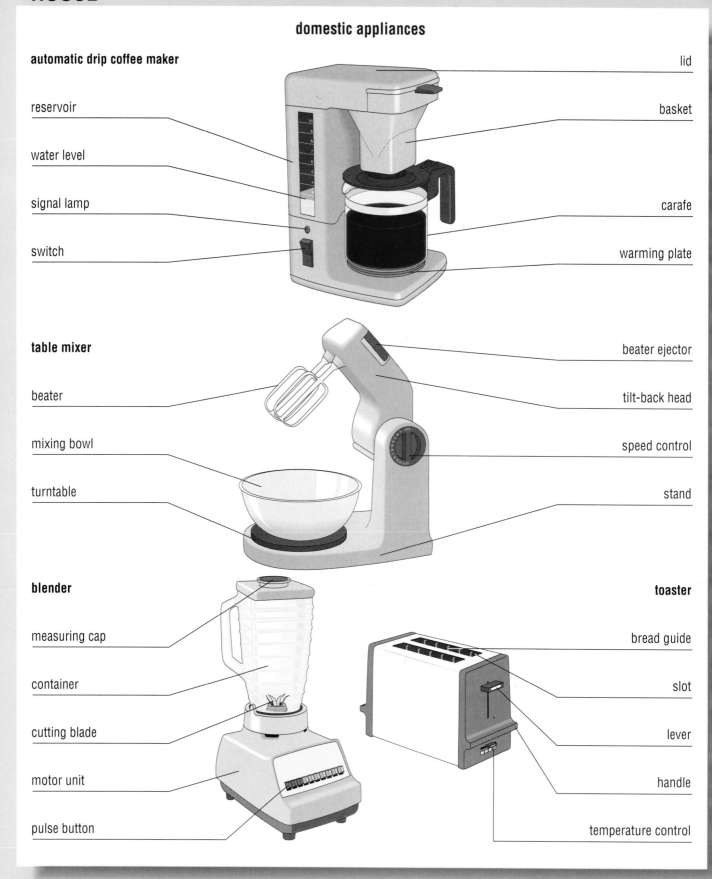

automatic drip coffee maker

reservoir

water level

signal lamp

switch

lid

basket

carafe

warming plate

table mixer

beater

mixing bowl

turntable

beater ejector

tilt-back head

speed control

stand

blender

measuring cap

container

cutting blade

motor unit

pulse button

toaster

bread guide

slot

lever

handle

temperature control

electric range

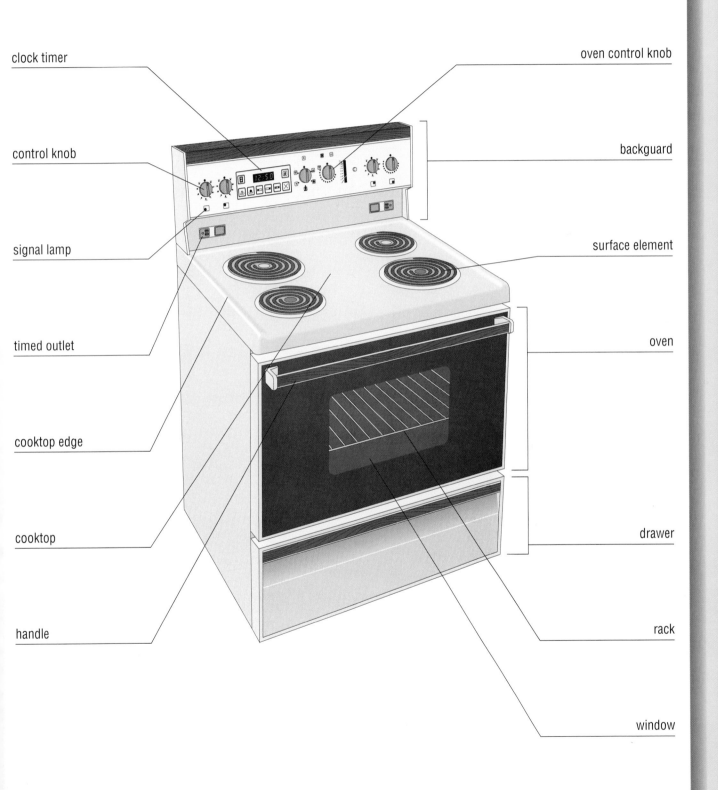

clock timer

control knob

signal lamp

timed outlet

cooktop edge

cooktop

handle

oven control knob

backguard

surface element

oven

drawer

rack

window

refrigerator

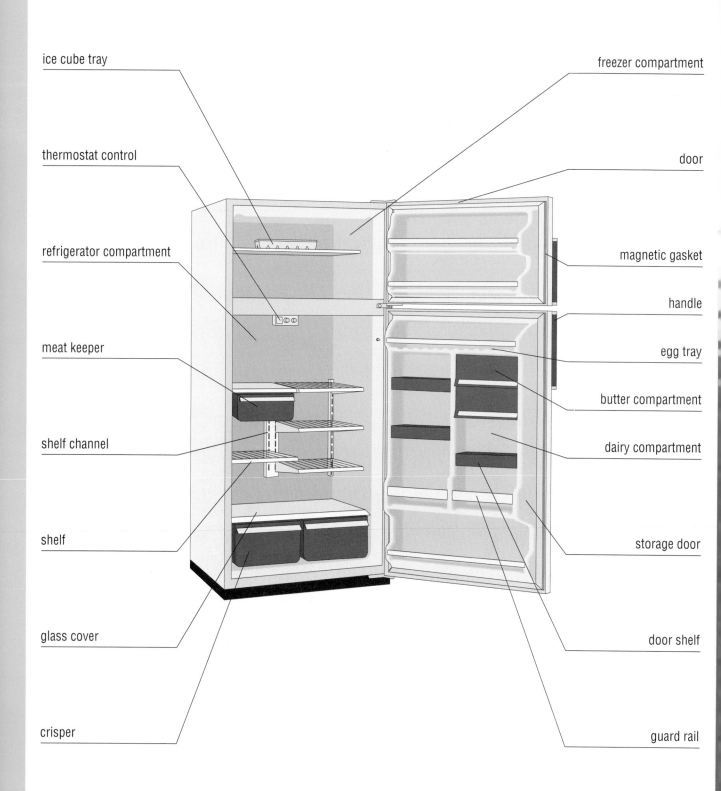

ice cube tray

thermostat control

refrigerator compartment

meat keeper

shelf channel

shelf

glass cover

crisper

freezer compartment

door

magnetic gasket

handle

egg tray

butter compartment

dairy compartment

storage door

door shelf

guard rail

plane surfaces

triangle

circle

square

rhombus

trapezoid

parallelogram

rectangle

solids

cylinder

sphere

cone

prism

pyramid

cube

parallelepiped

solar spectrum

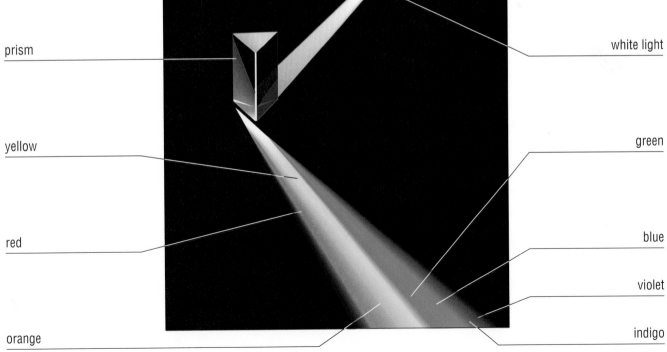

prism

white light

yellow

green

red

blue

violet

orange

indigo

SCHOOL

school supplies

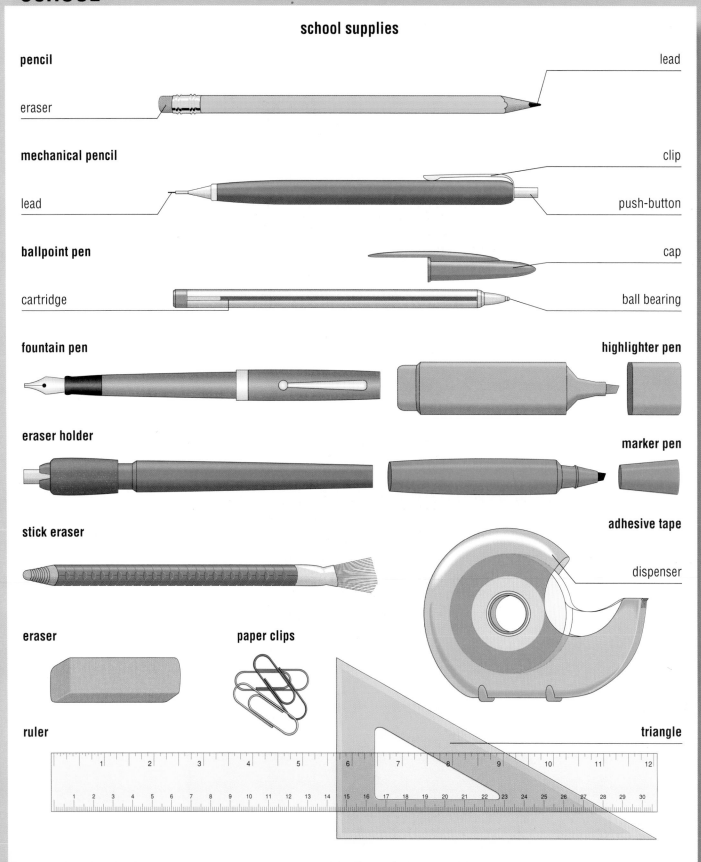

pencil — lead

eraser

mechanical pencil — clip

lead — push-button

ballpoint pen — cap

cartridge — ball bearing

fountain pen

highlighter pen

eraser holder

marker pen

stick eraser

adhesive tape

dispenser

eraser

paper clips

ruler

triangle

72

school supplies

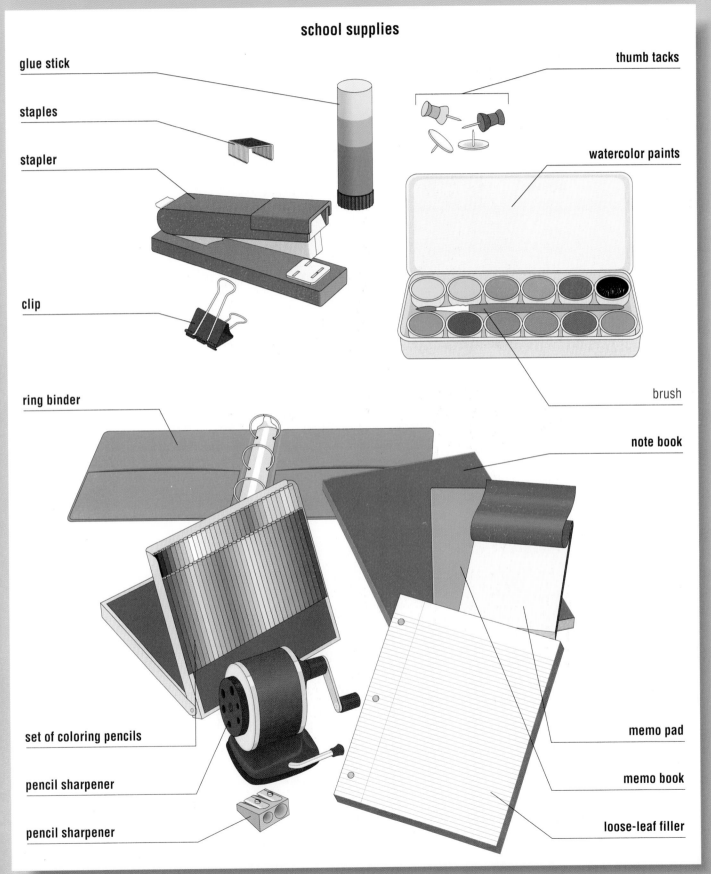

glue stick

thumb tacks

staples

stapler

watercolor paints

clip

brush

ring binder

note book

set of coloring pencils

pencil sharpener

memo pad

memo book

pencil sharpener

loose-leaf filler

microcomputer

display

central processing unit

microprocessor

keyboard cable

keyboard

printed document

disk drive

printer

floppydisk

mouse

pocket calculator

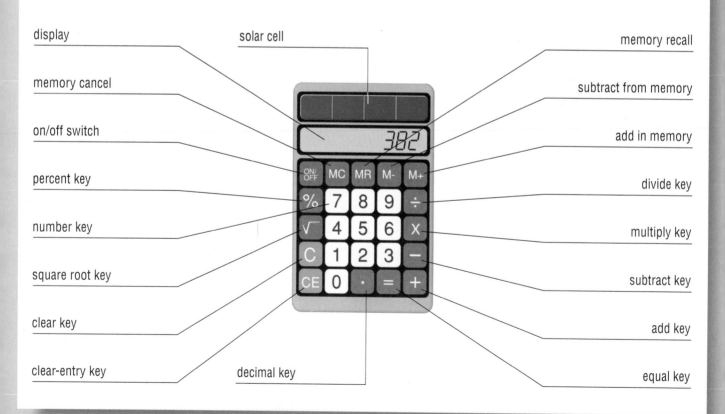

display

memory cancel

on/off switch

percent key

number key

square root key

clear key

clear-entry key

solar cell

decimal key

memory recall

subtract from memory

add in memory

divide key

multiply key

subtract key

add key

equal key

carpentry

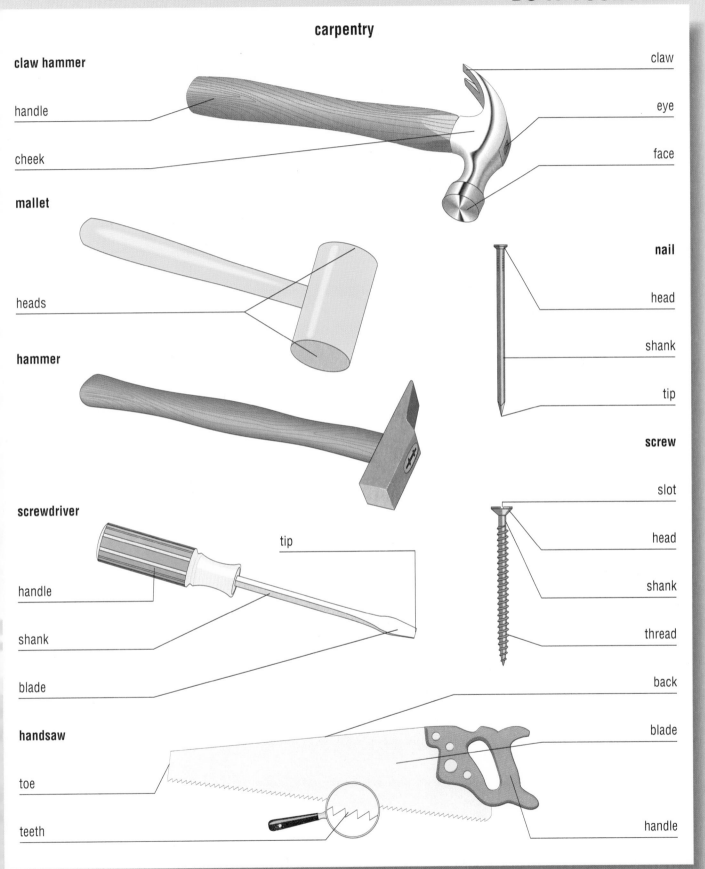

claw hammer

handle

cheek

claw

eye

face

mallet

heads

nail

head

shank

tip

hammer

screw

slot

head

shank

thread

screwdriver

handle

shank

blade

tip

back

blade

handle

handsaw

toe

teeth

DO-IT-YOURSELF

tools

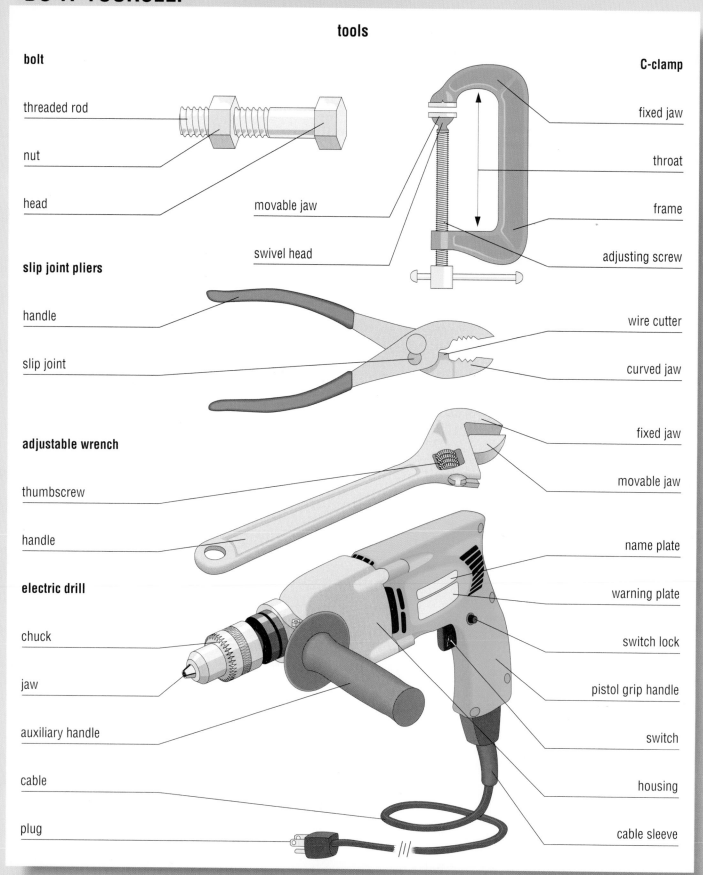

bolt

threaded rod

nut

head

C-clamp

fixed jaw

throat

frame

adjusting screw

movable jaw

swivel head

slip joint pliers

handle

slip joint

wire cutter

curved jaw

adjustable wrench

thumbscrew

handle

fixed jaw

movable jaw

electric drill

chuck

jaw

auxiliary handle

cable

plug

name plate

warning plate

switch lock

pistol grip handle

switch

housing

cable sleeve

painting upkeep

paint roller

roller frame

roller cover

tray

brush

handle

ferrule

bristles

scraper

removable blade

knurled bolt

handle

extension ladder

rung

side rail

pulley

locking device

hoisting rope

stepladder

tool tray

brace

step

platform ladder

safety rail

shelf

platform

step

anti-slip shoe

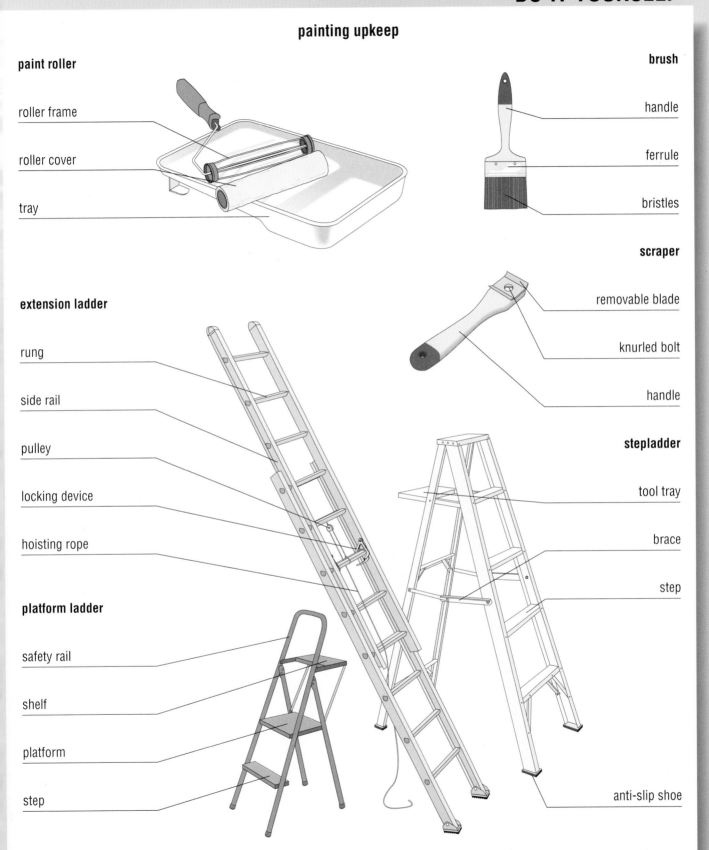

running shoe

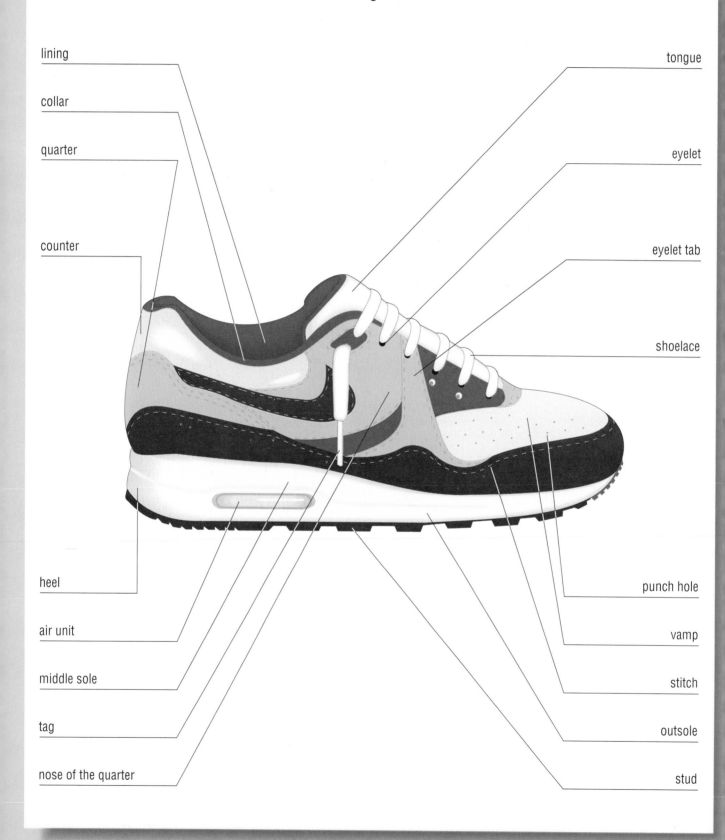

lining

collar

quarter

counter

heel

air unit

middle sole

tag

nose of the quarter

tongue

eyelet

eyelet tab

shoelace

punch hole

vamp

stitch

outsole

stud

men's clothing

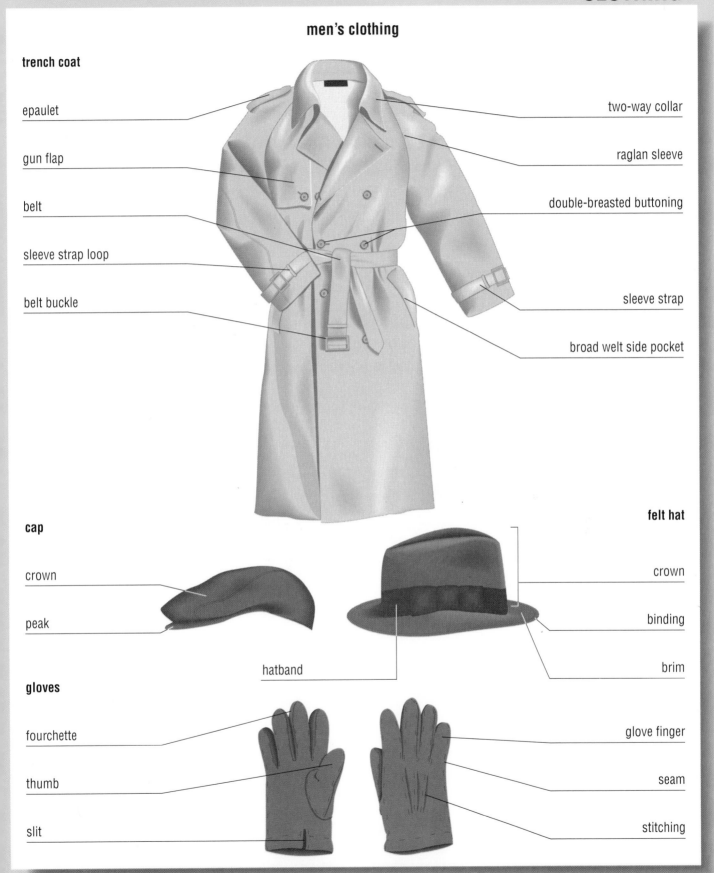

trench coat

epaulet

gun flap

belt

sleeve strap loop

belt buckle

two-way collar

raglan sleeve

double-breasted buttoning

sleeve strap

broad welt side pocket

cap

crown

peak

felt hat

crown

binding

brim

hatband

gloves

fourchette

thumb

slit

glove finger

seam

stitching

CLOTHING

men's clothing

single-breasted coat

single-breasted coat

top collar

notch

lapel

shirt

flap pocket

vest

necktie

pocket handkerchief

watch pocket

breast welt pocket

shirt cuff

shirttail

pants

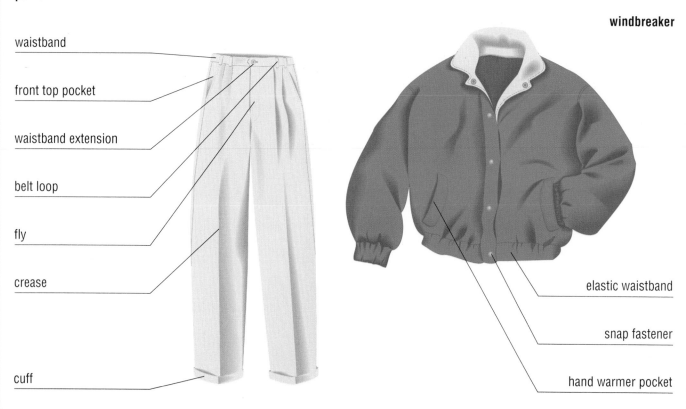

waistband

front top pocket

waistband extension

belt loop

fly

crease

cuff

windbreaker

elastic waistband

snap fastener

hand warmer pocket

sweaters

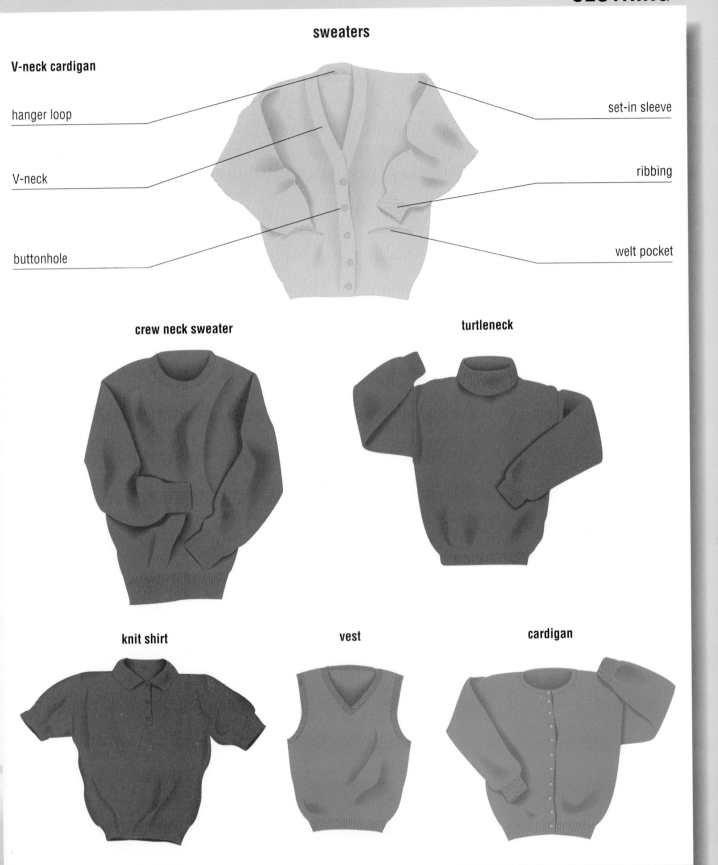

V-neck cardigan

hanger loop

V-neck

buttonhole

set-in sleeve

ribbing

welt pocket

crew neck sweater

turtleneck

knit shirt

vest

cardigan

CLOTHING

women's clothing

coats

jacket

car coat

overcoat

blouses

classic blouse

wrap-over top

body suit

skirts

pleated skirt

straight skirt

culotte

children's clothing

sleeper

- set-in sleeve
- ribbing
- screen print
- snap-fastening front
- inside-leg snap-fastening
- vinyl grip sole

overall

- strap
- buckle
- T-shirt
- pocket
- patch pocket
- bib
- lining

shirt

- breast pocket
- buttoned placket

jeans

- fob pocket
- belt
- front top pocket
- handkerchief
- top stitching
- fly

Bermuda shorts

- waistband
- dart

CLOTHING

personal articles

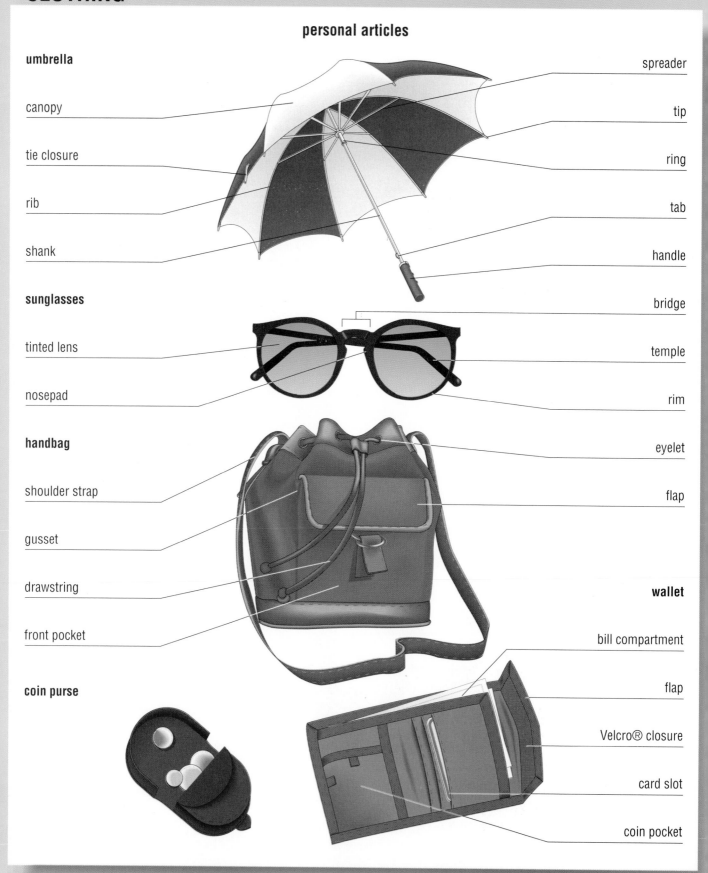

umbrella

canopy

tie closure

rib

shank

spreader

tip

ring

tab

handle

bridge

sunglasses

tinted lens

nosepad

temple

rim

handbag

shoulder strap

gusset

drawstring

front pocket

eyelet

flap

wallet

bill compartment

flap

coin purse

Velcro® closure

card slot

coin pocket

telephone set

telephone/answering system

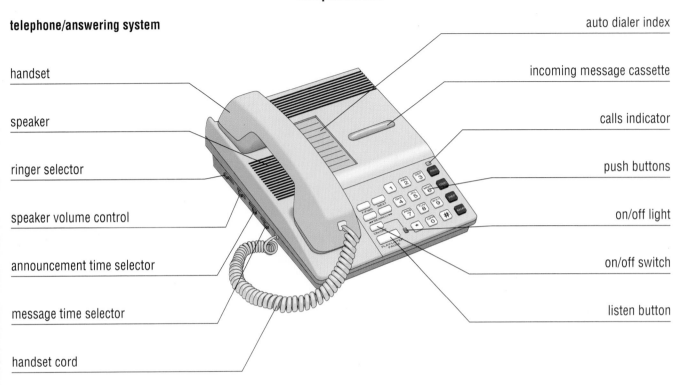

handset

speaker

ringer selector

speaker volume control

announcement time selector

message time selector

handset cord

auto dialer index

incoming message cassette

calls indicator

push buttons

on/off light

on/off switch

listen button

coinbox telephone

coin return knob

coin slot

coin return bucket

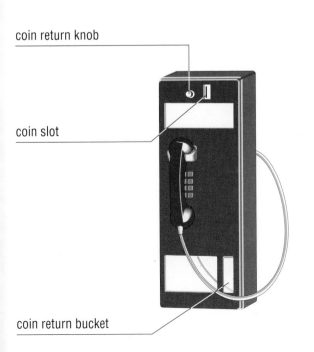

portable cellular telephone

push-button telephone

cordless telephone

COMMUNICATIONS

AM-FM cassette player

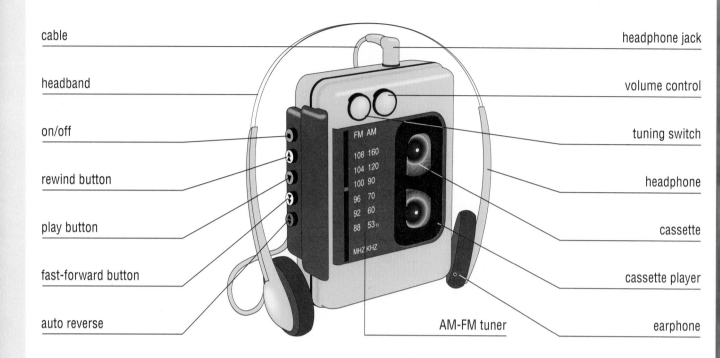

cable

headband

on/off

rewind button

play button

fast-forward button

auto reverse

headphone jack

volume control

tuning switch

headphone

cassette

cassette player

AM-FM tuner

earphone

AM-FM cassette recorder

mode selectors

stereo control

on/off/volume

handle

antenna

cassette player controls

tone controls

tuning switch

speaker

AM-FM tuner

cassette

cassette player

camera

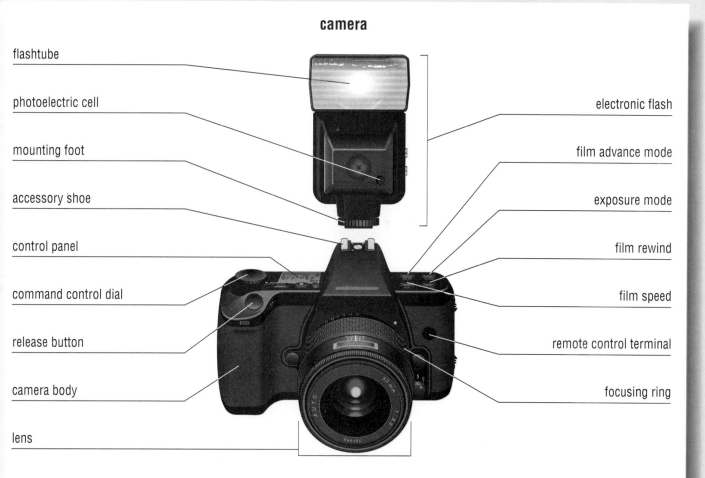

flashtube

photoelectric cell

mounting foot

accessory shoe

control panel

command control dial

release button

camera body

lens

electronic flash

film advance mode

exposure mode

film rewind

film speed

remote control terminal

focusing ring

slide projector

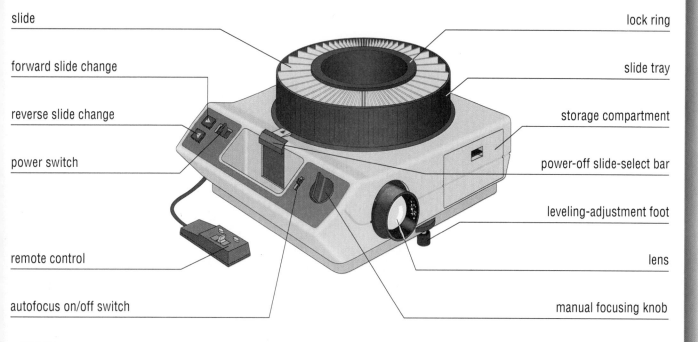

slide

forward slide change

reverse slide change

power switch

remote control

autofocus on/off switch

lock ring

slide tray

storage compartment

power-off slide-select bar

leveling-adjustment foot

lens

manual focusing knob

COMMUNICATIONS

television set

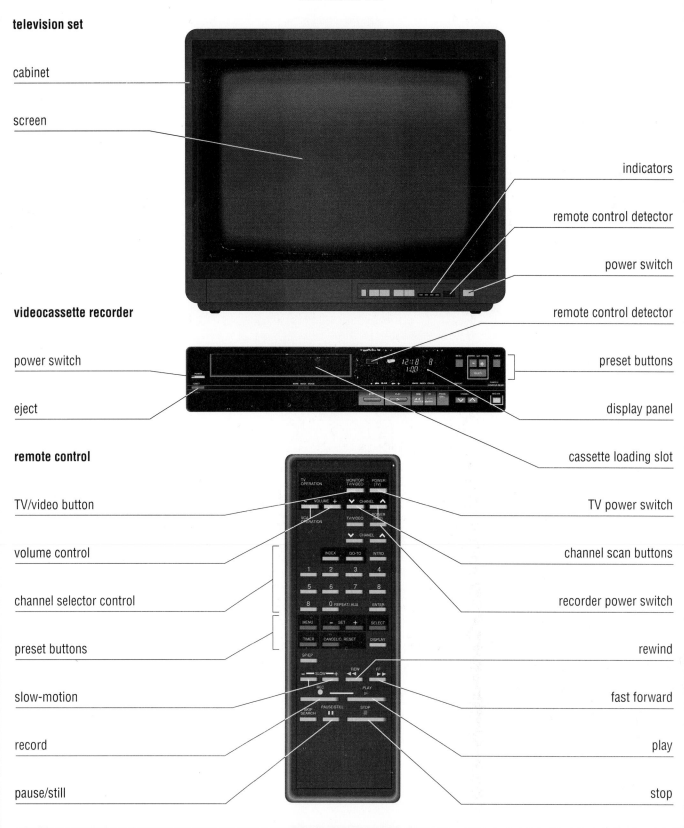

television set

cabinet

screen

indicators

remote control detector

power switch

videocassette recorder

remote control detector

power switch

preset buttons

eject

display panel

cassette loading slot

remote control

TV/video button

TV power switch

volume control

channel scan buttons

channel selector control

recorder power switch

preset buttons

rewind

slow-motion

fast forward

record

play

pause/still

stop

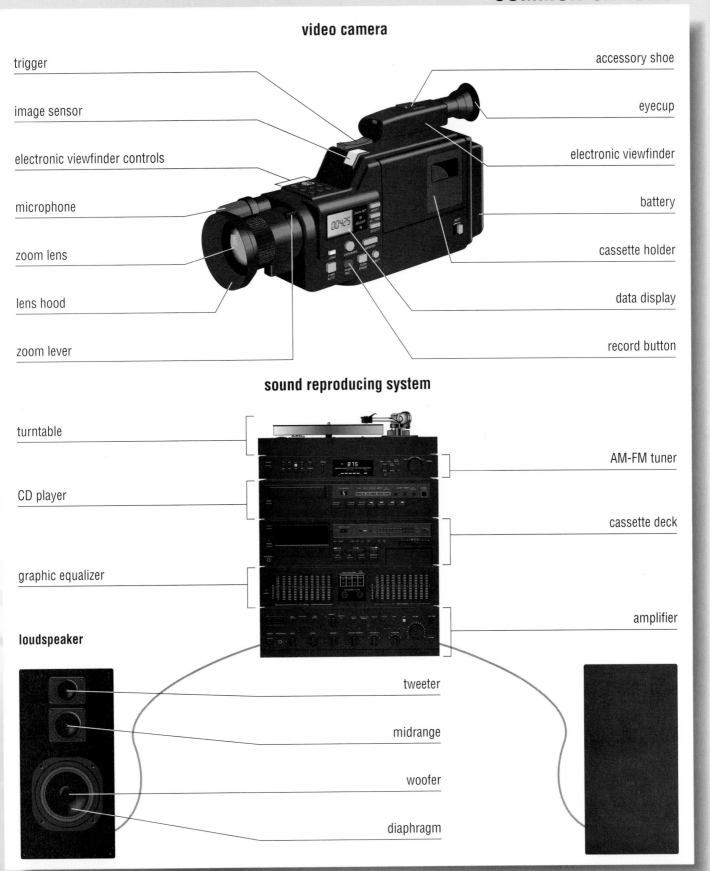

video camera

trigger

image sensor

electronic viewfinder controls

microphone

zoom lens

lens hood

zoom lever

accessory shoe

eyecup

electronic viewfinder

battery

cassette holder

data display

record button

sound reproducing system

turntable

CD player

graphic equalizer

loudspeaker

AM-FM tuner

cassette deck

amplifier

tweeter

midrange

woofer

diaphragm

automobile

body

antenna

sliding roof

windshield

windshield wiper

outside mirror

hood

grille

headlight

bumper

shield

wheel

gas tank door

trunk

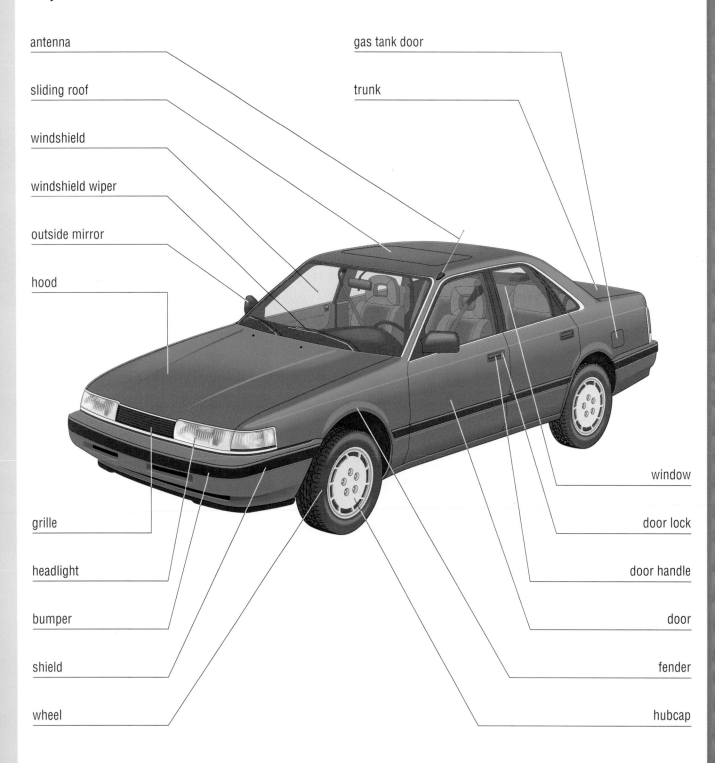

window

door lock

door handle

door

fender

hubcap

automobile

dashboard

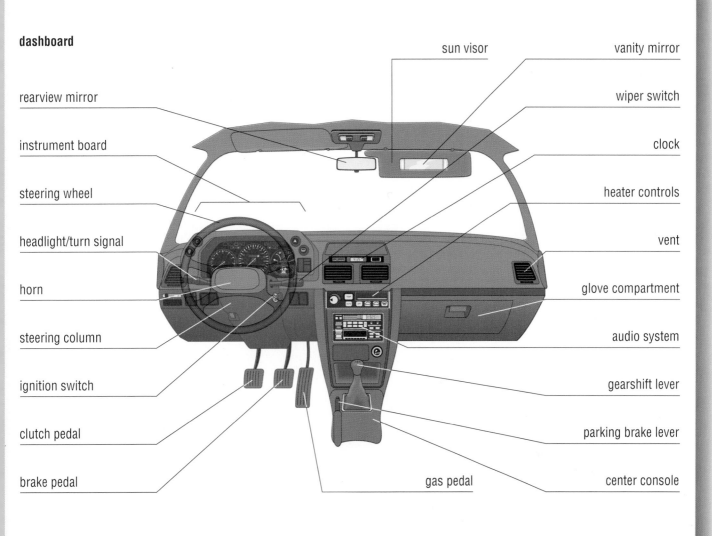

sun visor

vanity mirror

rearview mirror

wiper switch

instrument board

clock

steering wheel

heater controls

headlight/turn signal

vent

horn

glove compartment

steering column

audio system

ignition switch

gearshift lever

clutch pedal

parking brake lever

brake pedal

gas pedal

center console

instrument board

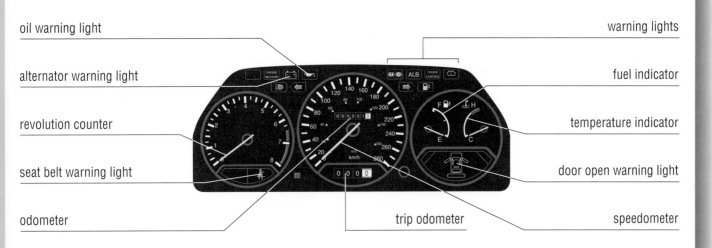

oil warning light

warning lights

alternator warning light

fuel indicator

revolution counter

temperature indicator

seat belt warning light

door open warning light

odometer

trip odometer

speedometer

headlights

front headlights

rear headlights

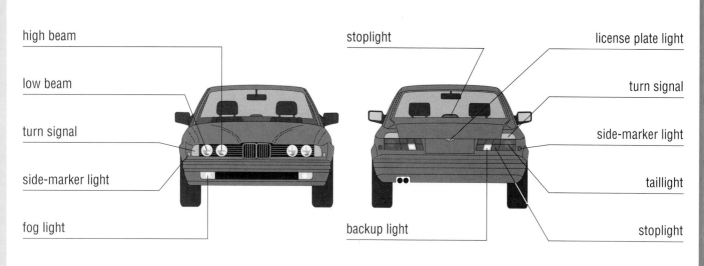

high beam

low beam

turn signal

side-marker light

fog light

stoplight

license plate light

turn signal

side-marker light

taillight

stoplight

backup light

types of bodies

four-door sedan

hatchback

two-door sedan

sports car

convertible

station wagon

pickup truck

multipurpose vehicle

minivan

limousine

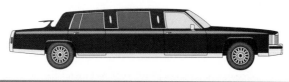

caravan

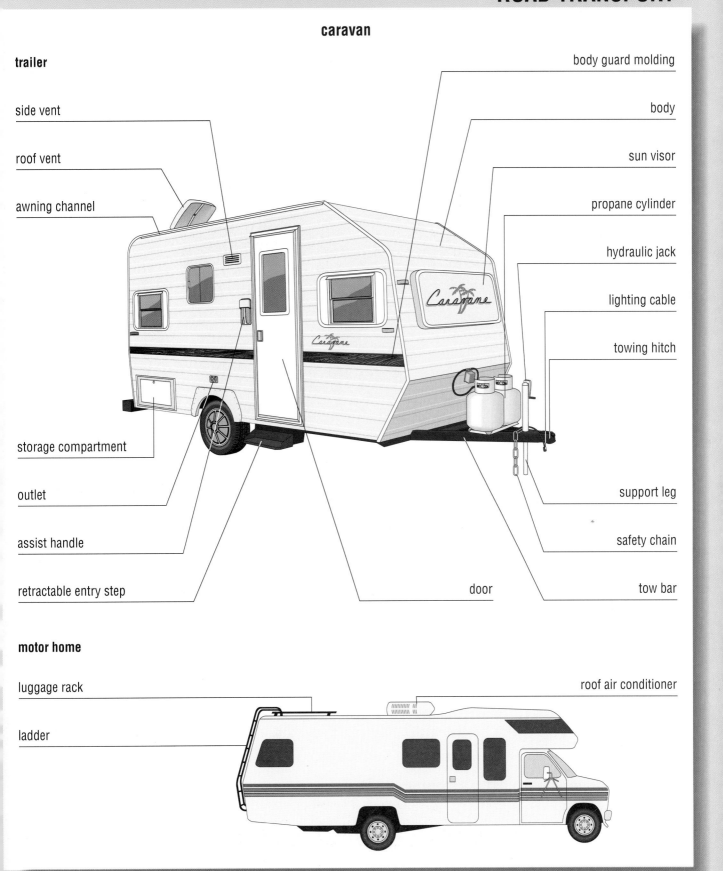

trailer

side vent

roof vent

awning channel

storage compartment

outlet

assist handle

retractable entry step

body guard molding

body

sun visor

propane cylinder

hydraulic jack

lighting cable

towing hitch

support leg

safety chain

door

tow bar

motor home

luggage rack

ladder

roof air conditioner

ROAD TRANSPORT

tractor

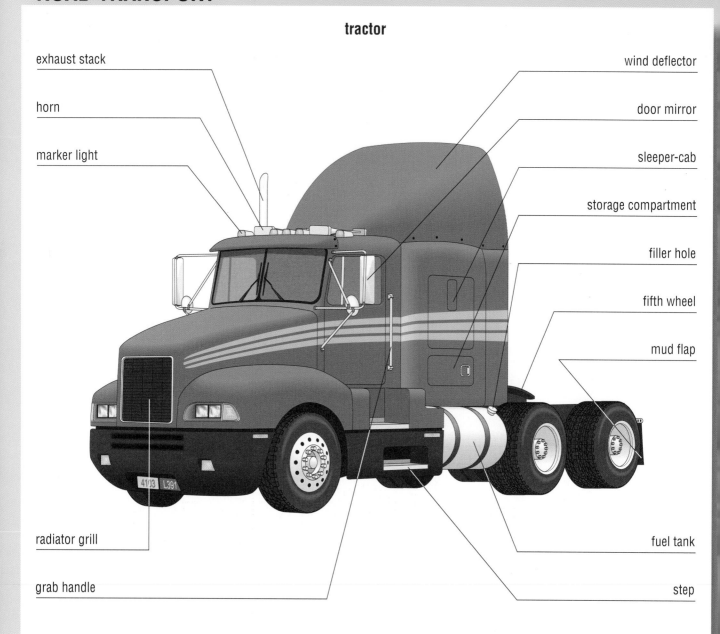

exhaust stack

horn

marker light

wind deflector

door mirror

sleeper-cab

storage compartment

filler hole

fifth wheel

mud flap

radiator grill

grab handle

fuel tank

step

articulated road train

truck tractor

truck trailer

semitrailer

motorcycle

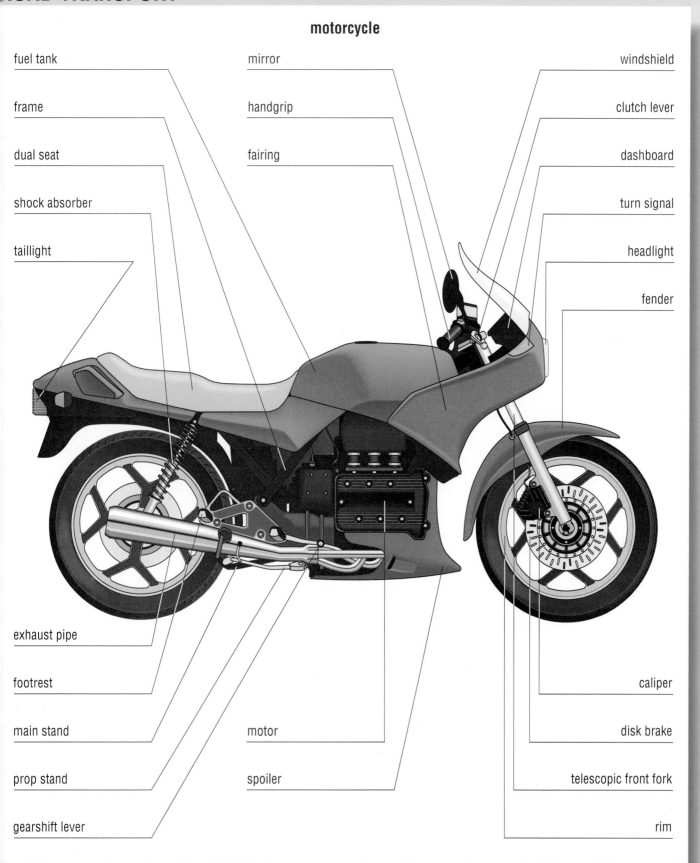

fuel tank

frame

dual seat

shock absorber

taillight

mirror

handgrip

fairing

windshield

clutch lever

dashboard

turn signal

headlight

fender

exhaust pipe

footrest

main stand

prop stand

gearshift lever

motor

spoiler

caliper

disk brake

telescopic front fork

rim

service station

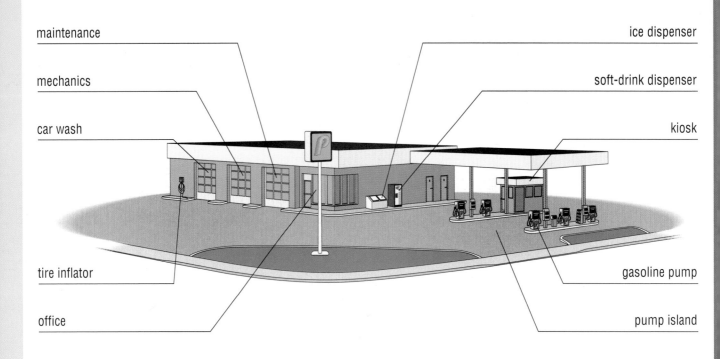

maintenance

mechanics

car wash

tire inflator

office

ice dispenser

soft-drink dispenser

kiosk

gasoline pump

pump island

gasoline pump

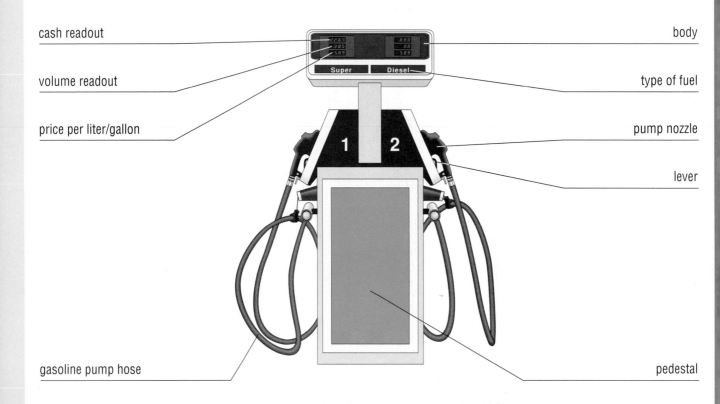

cash readout

volume readout

price per liter/gallon

gasoline pump hose

body

type of fuel

pump nozzle

lever

pedestal

bridges

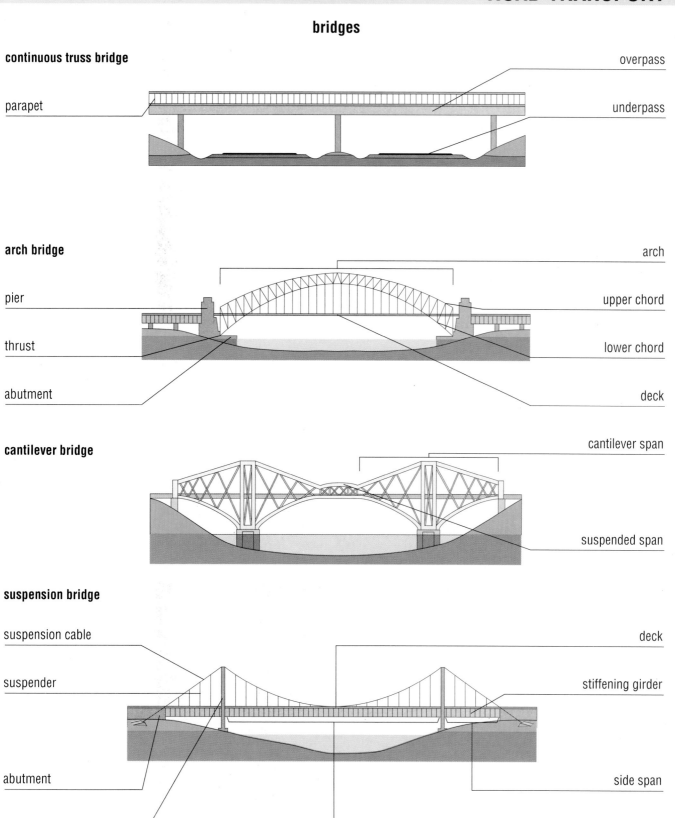

continuous truss bridge

overpass

parapet

underpass

arch bridge

arch

pier

upper chord

thrust

lower chord

abutment

deck

cantilever bridge

cantilever span

suspended span

suspension bridge

suspension cable

deck

suspender

stiffening girder

abutment

side span

tower

center span

bicycle

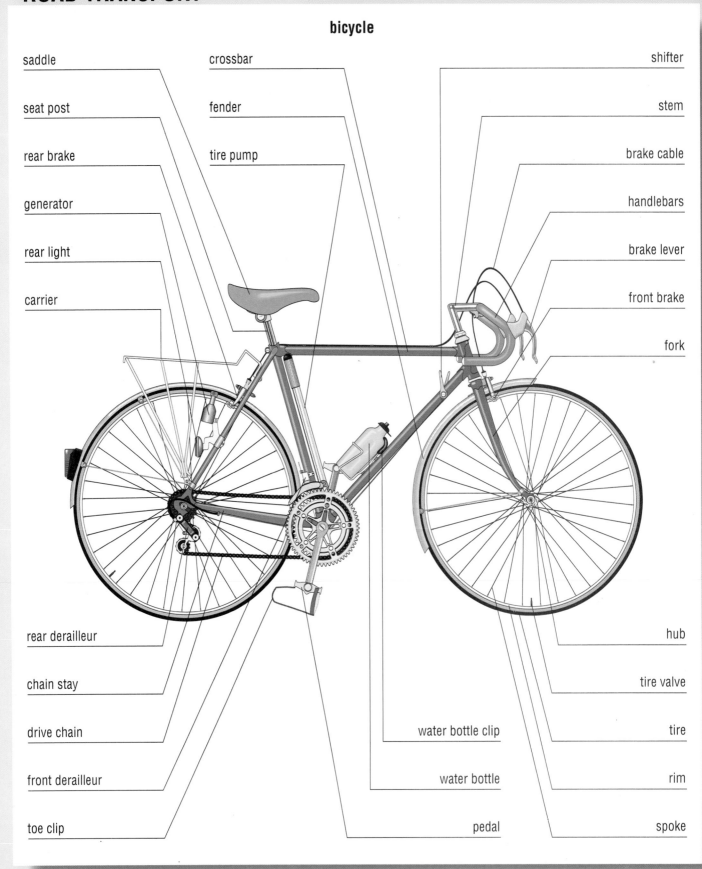

saddle

seat post

rear brake

generator

rear light

carrier

crossbar

fender

tire pump

shifter

stem

brake cable

handlebars

brake lever

front brake

fork

rear derailleur

chain stay

drive chain

front derailleur

toe clip

water bottle clip

water bottle

pedal

hub

tire valve

tire

rim

spoke

bicycle

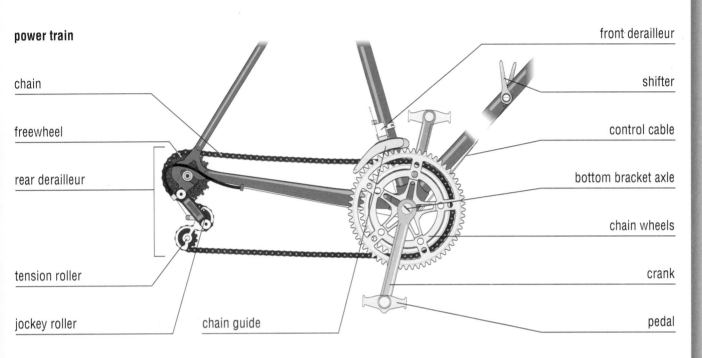

power train

chain

freewheel

rear derailleur

tension roller

jockey roller

chain guide

front derailleur

shifter

control cable

bottom bracket axle

chain wheels

crank

pedal

protective helmet

lock

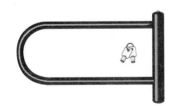

bicycle bag

RAIL TRANSPORT

high-speed train

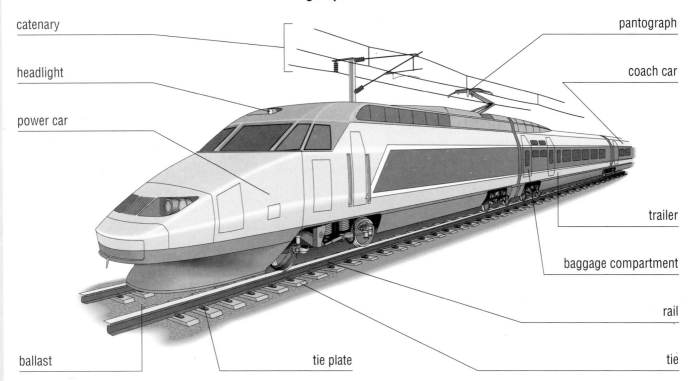

catenary

headlight

power car

pantograph

coach car

trailer

baggage compartment

rail

tie

ballast

tie plate

diesel-electric locomotive

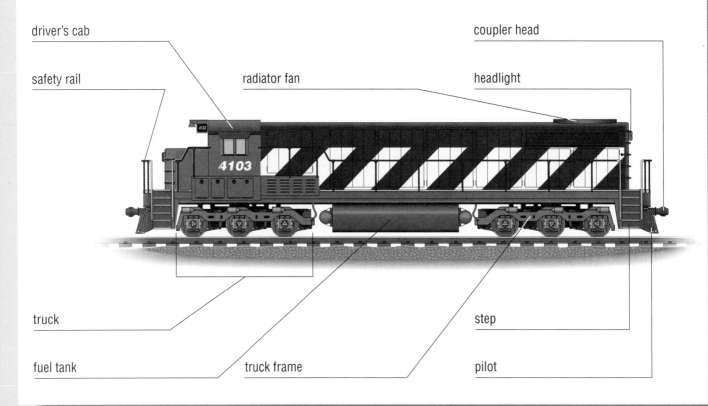

driver's cab

safety rail

radiator fan

coupler head

headlight

truck

fuel tank

truck frame

step

pilot

types of cars

hopper car

bulkhead flat car

depressed-center flat car

flat car

piggyback car

refrigerator car

tank car

automobile car

container car

livestock car

boxcar

gondola car

caboose

passenger liner

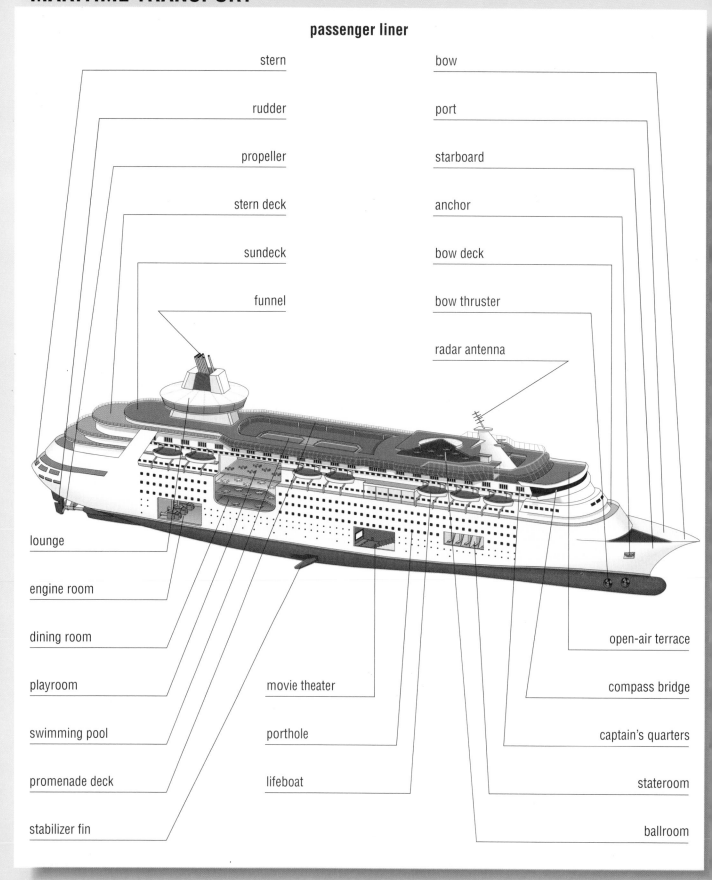

stern

bow

rudder

port

propeller

starboard

stern deck

anchor

sundeck

bow deck

funnel

bow thruster

radar antenna

lounge

engine room

dining room

open-air terrace

playroom

movie theater

compass bridge

swimming pool

porthole

captain's quarters

promenade deck

lifeboat

stateroom

stabilizer fin

ballroom

submarine

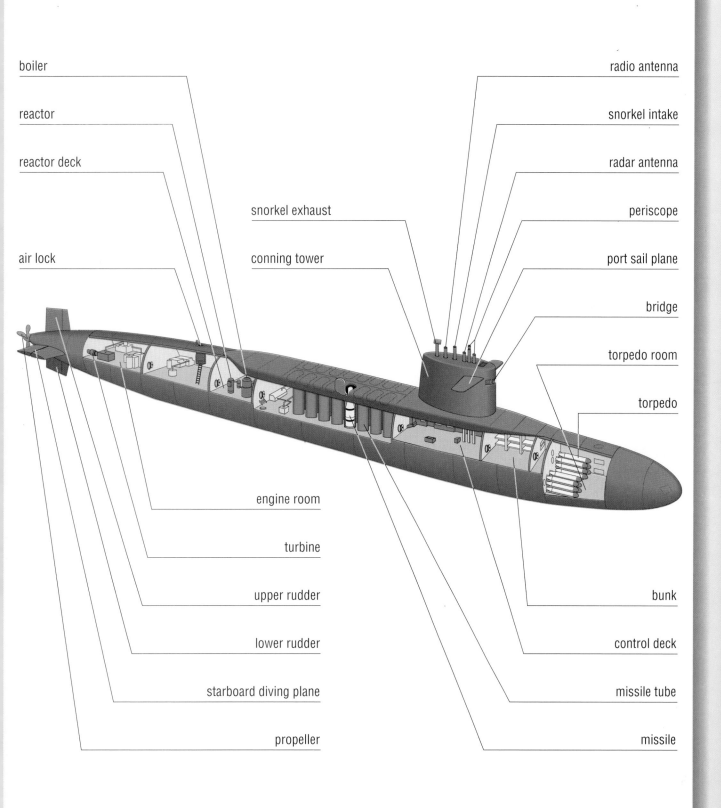

boiler

reactor

reactor deck

air lock

snorkel exhaust

conning tower

radio antenna

snorkel intake

radar antenna

periscope

port sail plane

bridge

torpedo room

torpedo

engine room

turbine

upper rudder

lower rudder

starboard diving plane

propeller

bunk

control deck

missile tube

missile

long-range jet

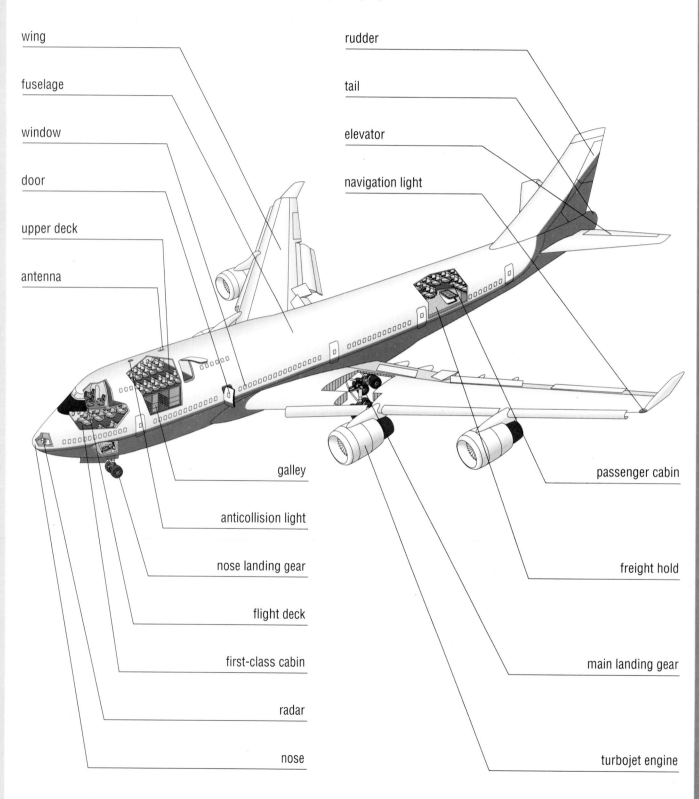

wing

fuselage

window

door

upper deck

antenna

rudder

tail

elevator

navigation light

galley

anticollision light

nose landing gear

flight deck

first-class cabin

radar

nose

passenger cabin

freight hold

main landing gear

turbojet engine

helicopter

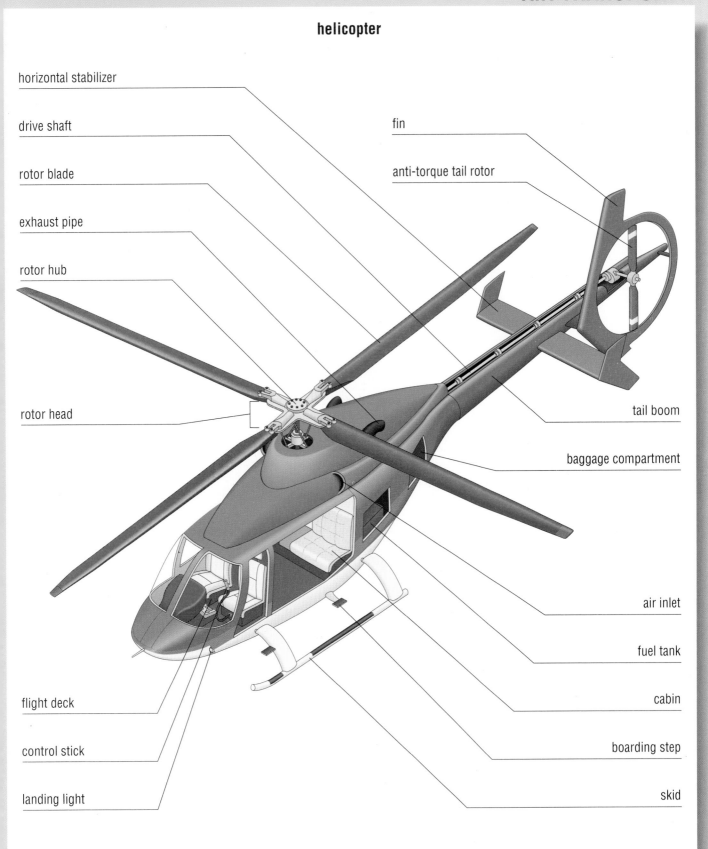

horizontal stabilizer

drive shaft

rotor blade

exhaust pipe

rotor hub

rotor head

fin

anti-torque tail rotor

tail boom

baggage compartment

air inlet

fuel tank

cabin

boarding step

skid

flight deck

control stick

landing light

rocket

launch escape system

command module

service module

lunar module

instrument unit

helium sphere

J-2 engine

liquid hydrogen tank

liquid oxygen tank

kerosene tank

stabilizing fin

F-1 engine

nozzle

payload

third stage

second stage

first stage

space shuttle

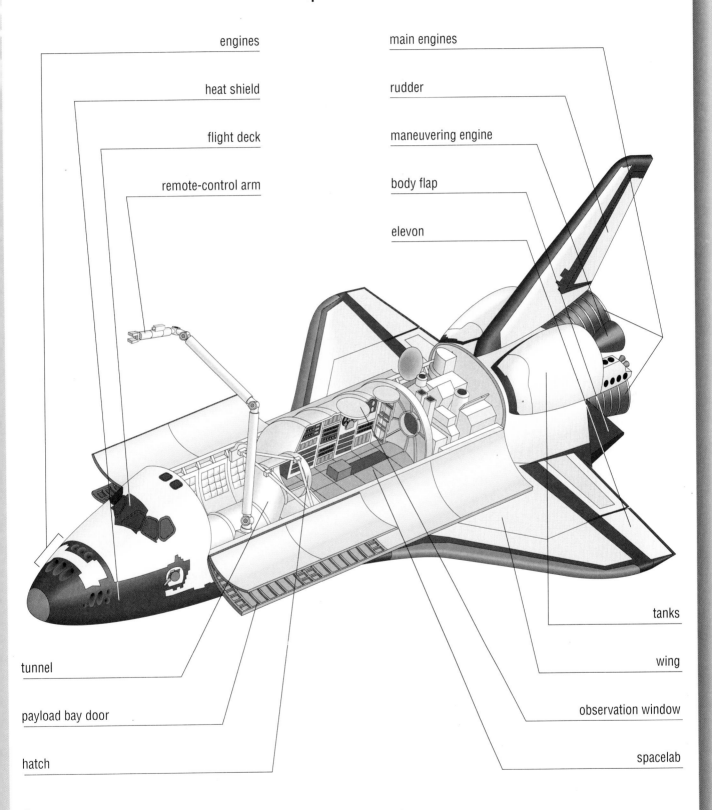

engines

heat shield

flight deck

remote-control arm

main engines

rudder

maneuvering engine

body flap

elevon

tanks

wing

observation window

tunnel

payload bay door

hatch

spacelab

armor

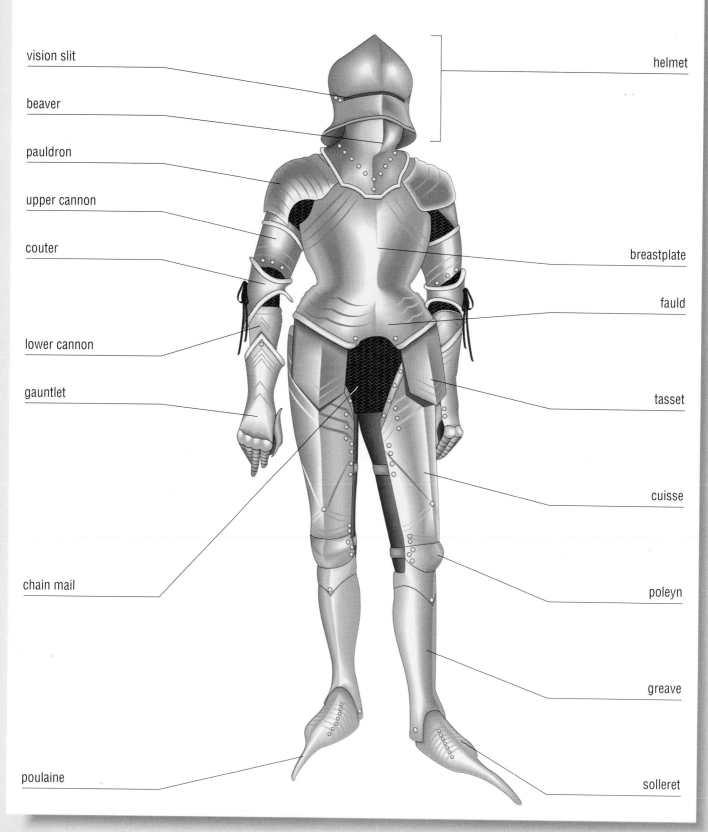

vision slit

beaver

pauldron

upper cannon

couter

lower cannon

gauntlet

chain mail

poulaine

helmet

breastplate

fauld

tasset

cuisse

poleyn

greave

solleret

thrusting and cutting weapons

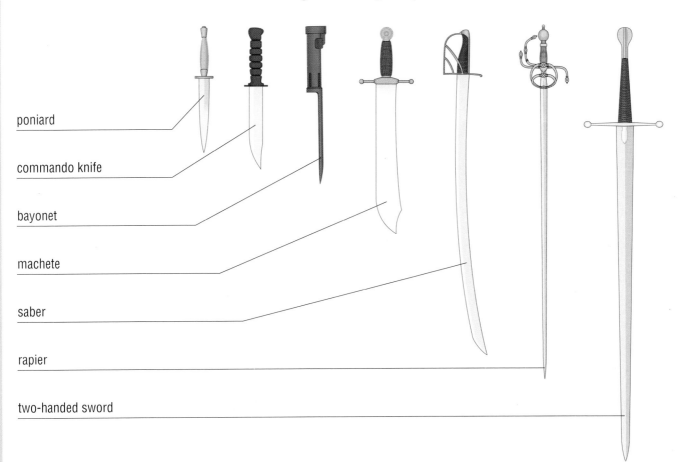

poniard

commando knife

bayonet

machete

saber

rapier

two-handed sword

crossbow

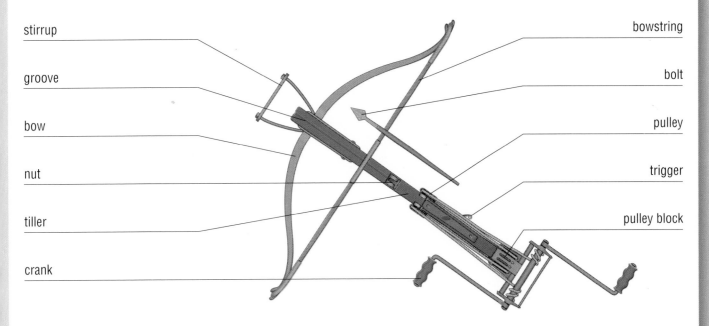

stirrup

groove

bow

nut

tiller

crank

bowstring

bolt

pulley

trigger

pulley block

WEAPONS

revolver

hammer

butt

front sight

muzzle

barrel

cylinder

loading gate

trigger guard

trigger

pistol

rear sight

hammer

magazine

magazine base

butt

barrel

front sight

slide

trigger guard

trigger

cartridge

magazine catch

tank

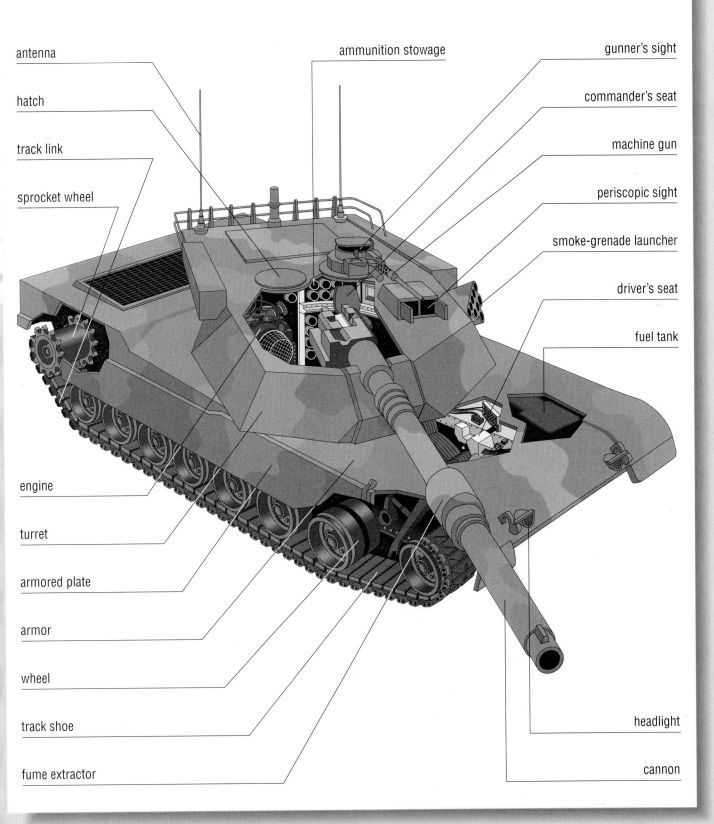

antenna

hatch

track link

sprocket wheel

ammunition stowage

gunner's sight

commander's seat

machine gun

periscopic sight

smoke-grenade launcher

driver's seat

fuel tank

engine

turret

armored plate

armor

wheel

track shoe

fume extractor

headlight

cannon

musical notation

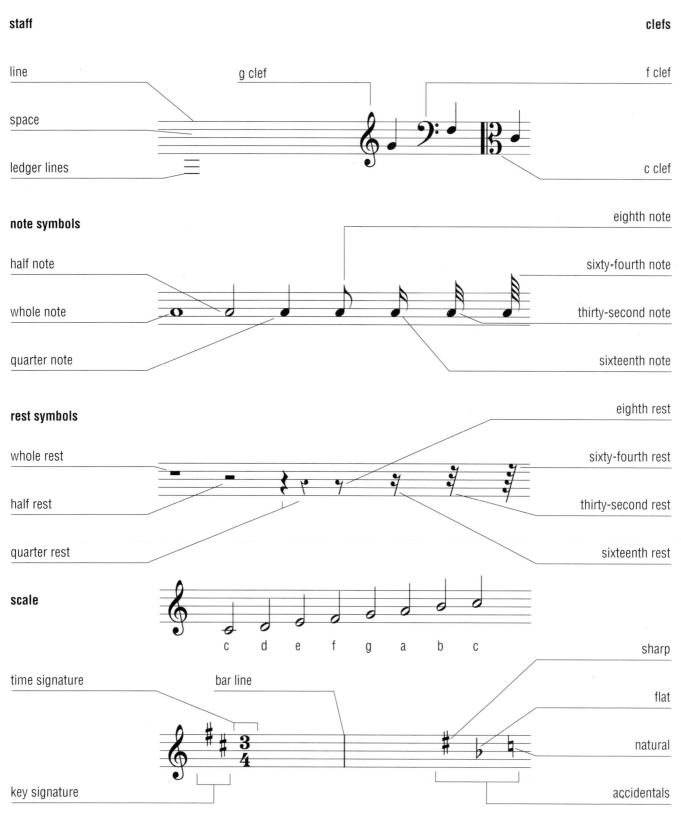

staff

line

space

ledger lines

g clef

clefs

f clef

c clef

note symbols

half note

whole note

quarter note

eighth note

sixty-fourth note

thirty-second note

sixteenth note

rest symbols

whole rest

half rest

quarter rest

eighth rest

sixty-fourth rest

thirty-second rest

sixteenth rest

scale

c d e f g a b c

time signature

bar line

key signature

sharp

flat

natural

accidentals

upright piano

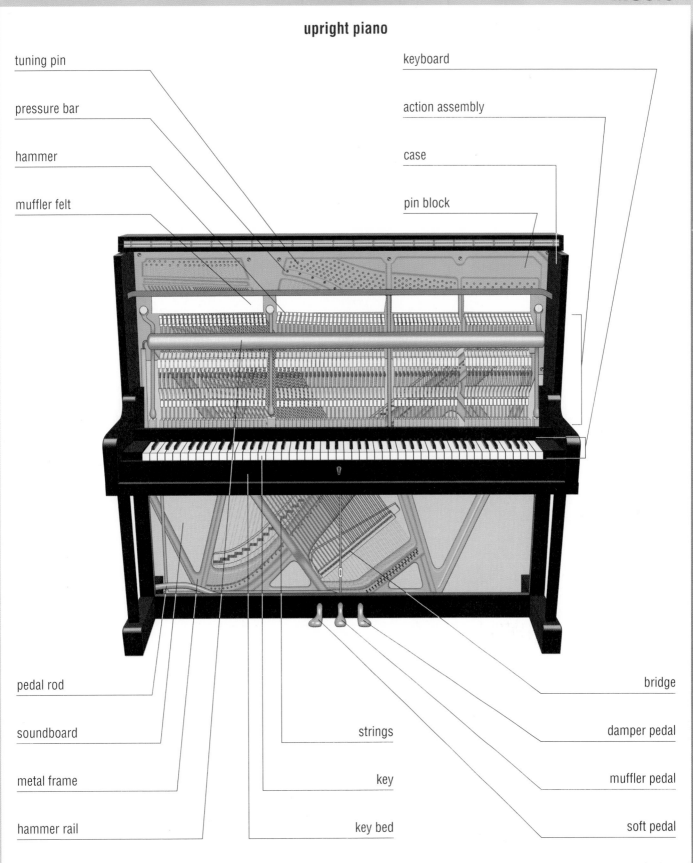

tuning pin

pressure bar

hammer

muffler felt

keyboard

action assembly

case

pin block

pedal rod

soundboard

metal frame

hammer rail

bridge

strings

damper pedal

key

muffler pedal

key bed

soft pedal

MUSIC

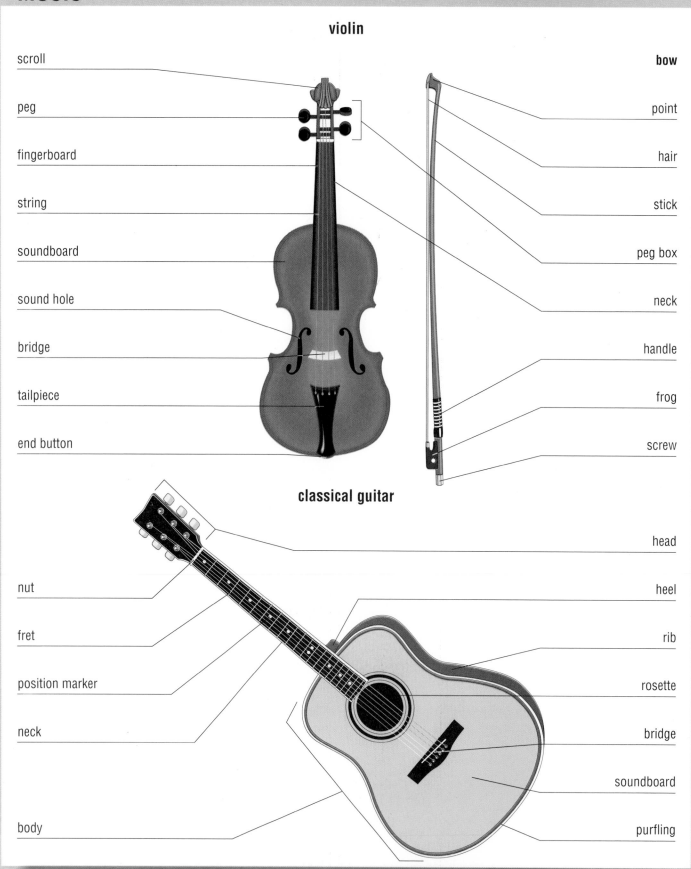

violin

scroll

peg

fingerboard

string

soundboard

sound hole

bridge

tailpiece

end button

bow

point

hair

stick

peg box

neck

handle

frog

screw

classical guitar

nut

fret

position marker

neck

body

head

heel

rib

rosette

bridge

soundboard

purfling

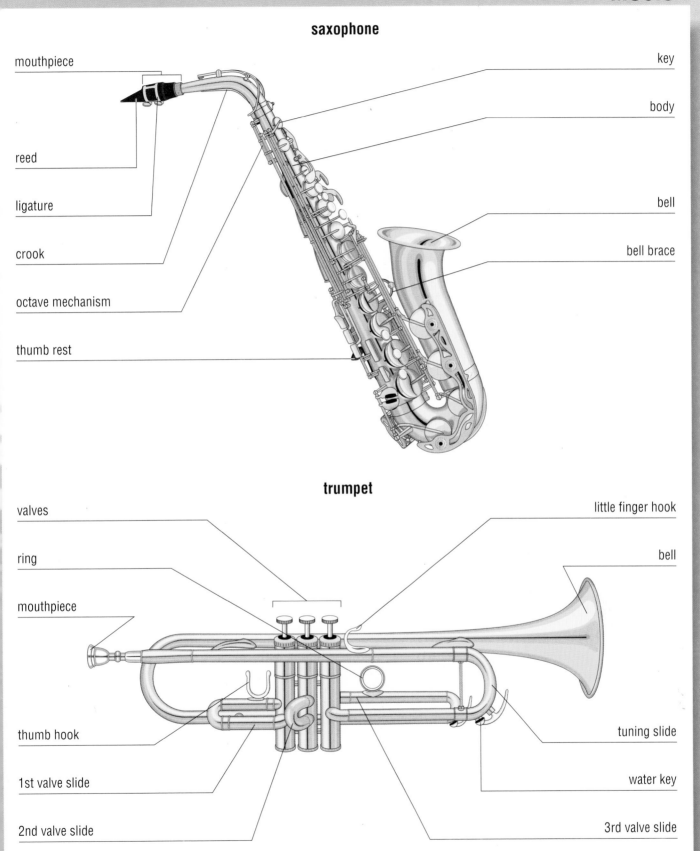

saxophone

mouthpiece

key

reed

body

ligature

crook

bell

bell brace

octave mechanism

thumb rest

trumpet

valves

little finger hook

ring

bell

mouthpiece

thumb hook

tuning slide

1st valve slide

water key

2nd valve slide

3rd valve slide

MUSIC

electric guitar

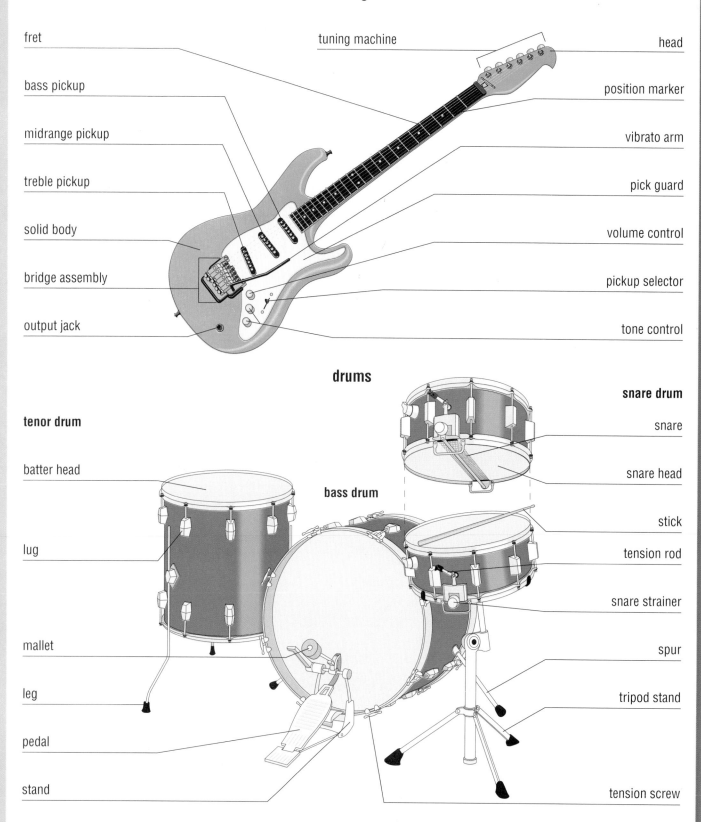

fret

bass pickup

midrange pickup

treble pickup

solid body

bridge assembly

output jack

tuning machine

head

position marker

vibrato arm

pick guard

volume control

pickup selector

tone control

drums

tenor drum

bass drum

snare drum

batter head

snare

snare head

lug

stick

mallet

tension rod

leg

snare strainer

pedal

spur

stand

tripod stand

tension screw

orchestra

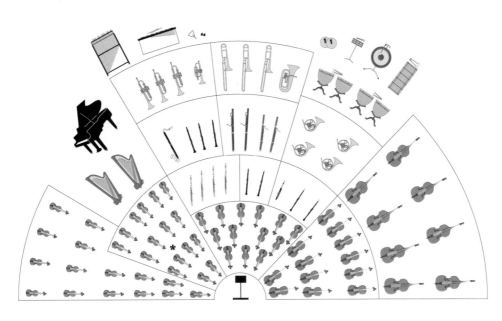

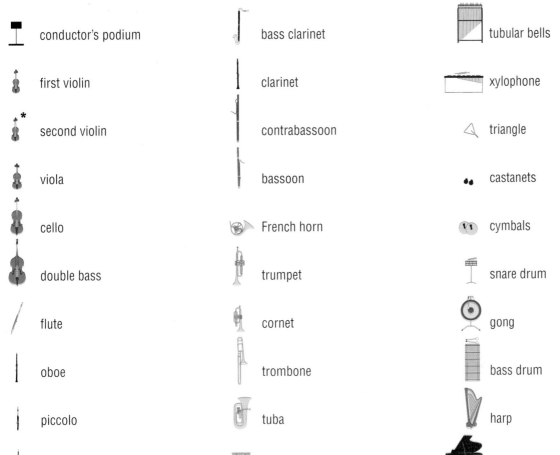

conductor's podium	bass clarinet	tubular bells
first violin	clarinet	xylophone
second violin *	contrabassoon	triangle
viola	bassoon	castanets
cello	French horn	cymbals
double bass	trumpet	snare drum
flute	cornet	gong
oboe	trombone	bass drum
piccolo	tuba	harp
English horn	timpani	piano

soccer

playing field

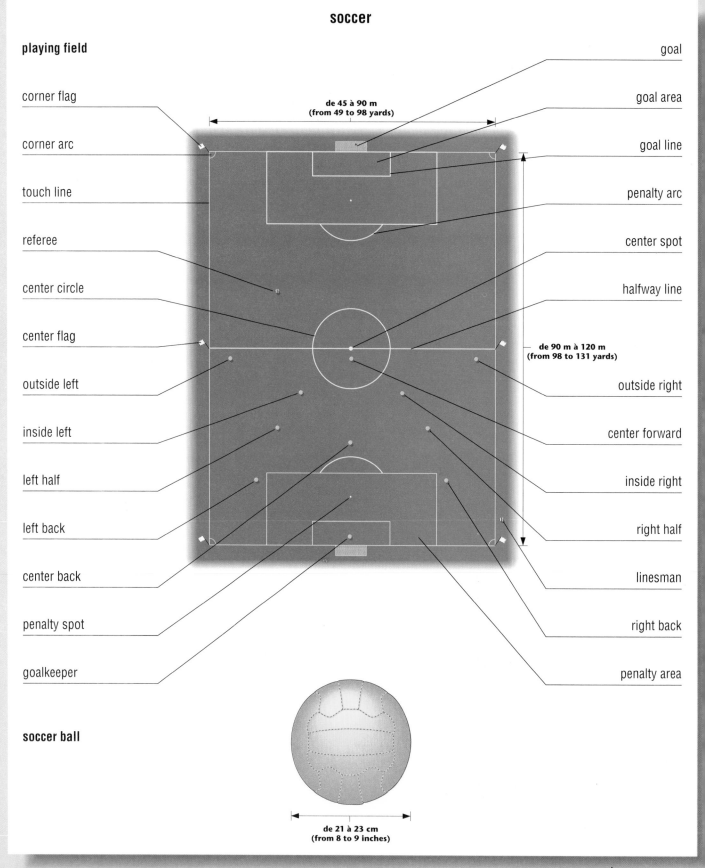

corner flag

corner arc

touch line

referee

center circle

center flag

outside left

inside left

left half

left back

center back

penalty spot

goalkeeper

goal

goal area

goal line

penalty arc

center spot

halfway line

outside right

center forward

inside right

right half

linesman

right back

penalty area

de 45 à 90 m
(from 49 to 98 yards)

de 90 m à 120 m
(from 98 to 131 yards)

soccer ball

de 21 à 23 cm
(from 8 to 9 inches)

rugby

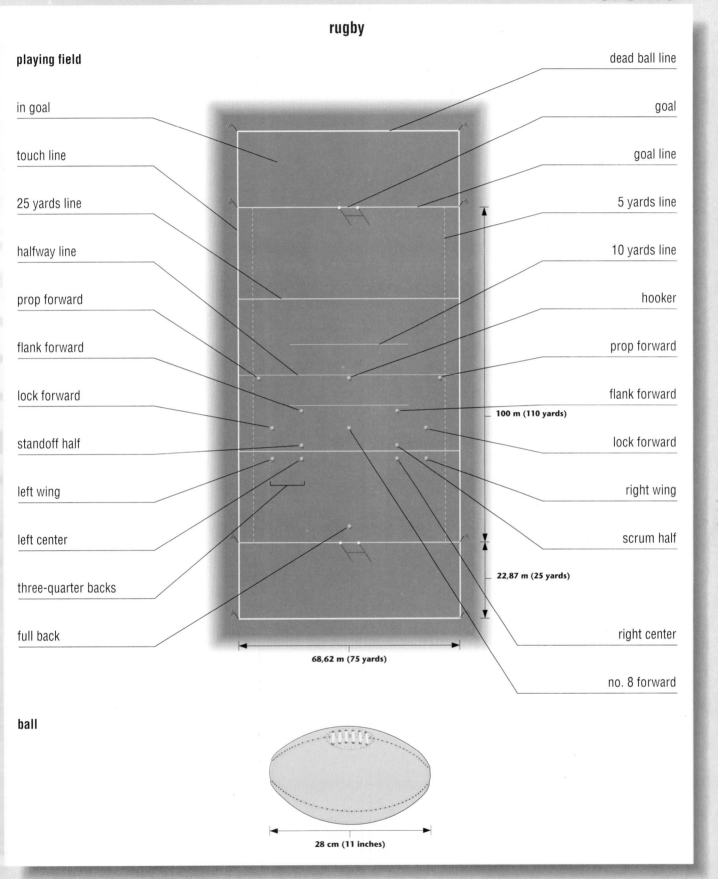

playing field

in goal

touch line

25 yards line

halfway line

prop forward

flank forward

lock forward

standoff half

left wing

left center

three-quarter backs

full back

dead ball line

goal

goal line

5 yards line

10 yards line

hooker

prop forward

flank forward

100 m (110 yards)

lock forward

right wing

scrum half

22,87 m (25 yards)

right center

no. 8 forward

68,62 m (75 yards)

ball

28 cm (11 inches)

SPORTS

football

tight end

left tackle

referee

left guard

left halfback

center

fullback

quarterback

right halfback

right guard

right tackle

neutral zone

split end

head linesman

line of scrimmage

end zone

line judge

right cornerback

outside linebacker

right defensive end

right safety

right defensive tackle

umpire

middle linebacker

left safety

back judge

left defensive tackle

inside linebacker

left defensive end

left cornerback

goal

goal line

football

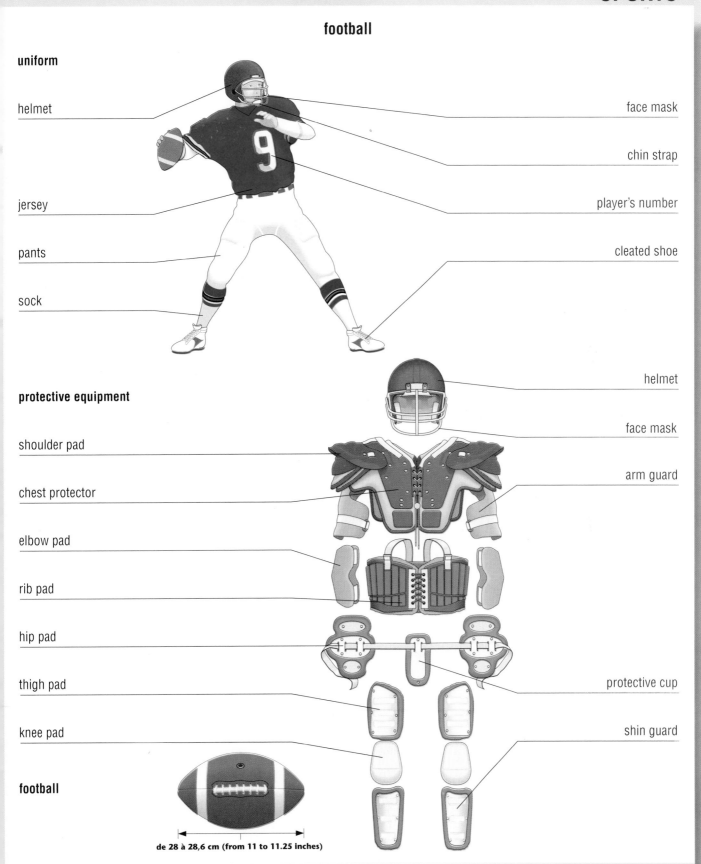

uniform

helmet

jersey

pants

sock

face mask

chin strap

player's number

cleated shoe

helmet

face mask

protective equipment

shoulder pad

chest protector

elbow pad

rib pad

hip pad

thigh pad

knee pad

arm guard

protective cup

shin guard

football

de 28 à 28,6 cm (from 11 to 11.25 inches)

baseball

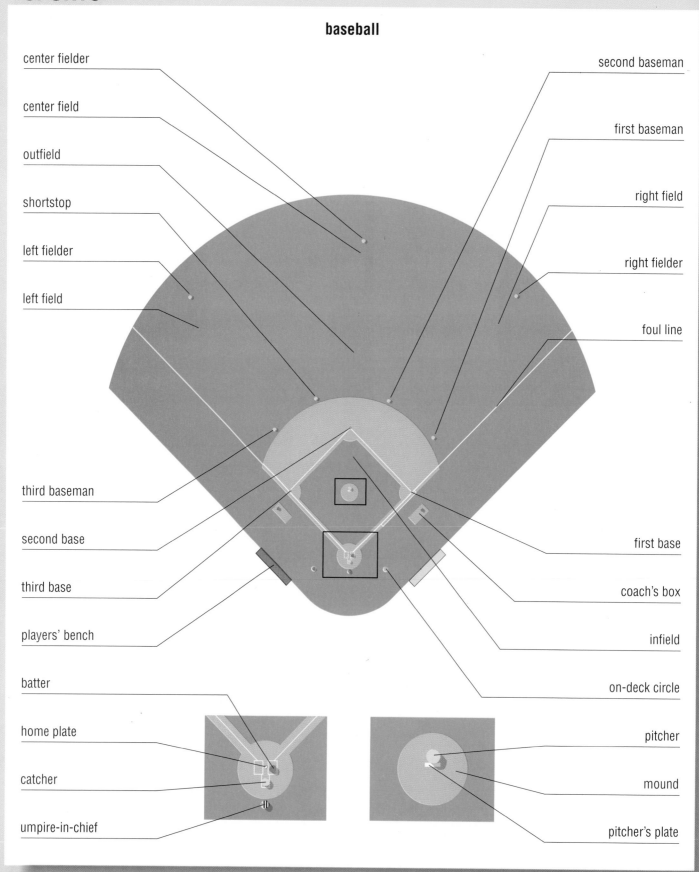

center fielder

center field

outfield

shortstop

left fielder

left field

third baseman

second base

third base

players' bench

batter

home plate

catcher

umpire-in-chief

second baseman

first baseman

right field

right fielder

foul line

first base

coach's box

infield

on-deck circle

pitcher

mound

pitcher's plate

baseball

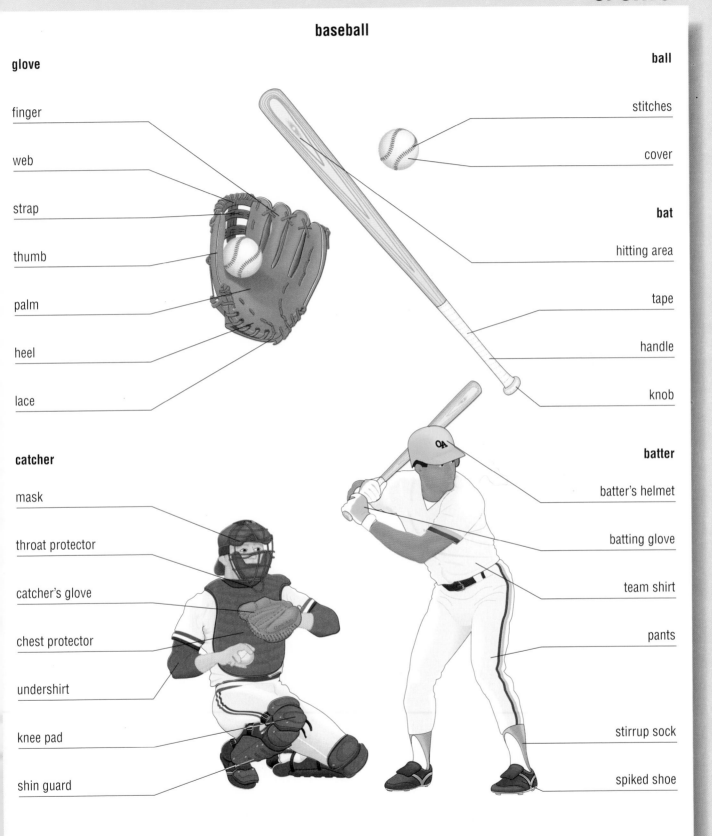

glove

finger

web

strap

thumb

palm

heel

lace

ball

stitches

cover

bat

hitting area

tape

handle

knob

catcher

mask

throat protector

catcher's glove

chest protector

undershirt

knee pad

shin guard

batter

batter's helmet

batting glove

team shirt

pants

stirrup sock

spiked shoe

cricket

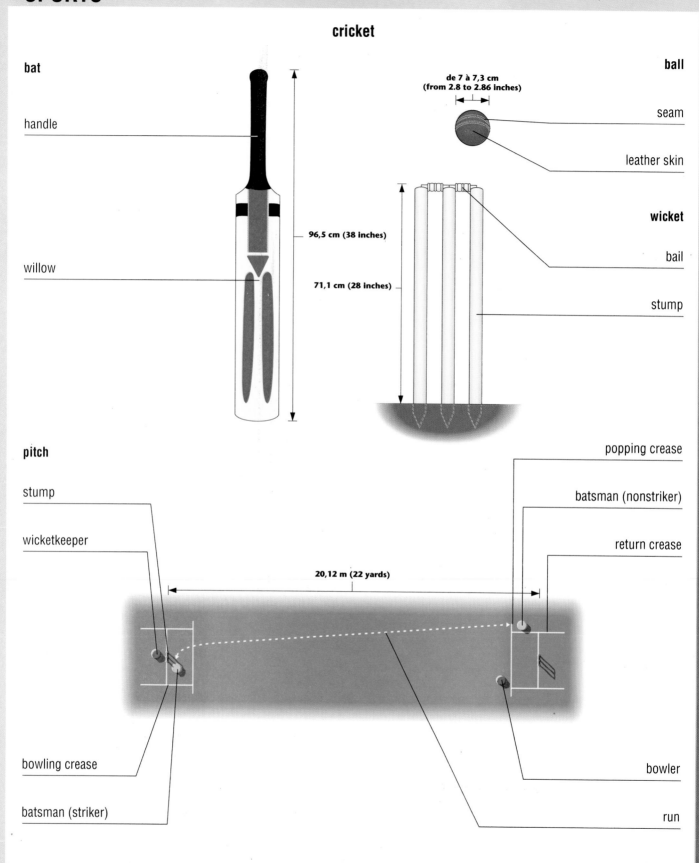

bat

handle

willow

96,5 cm (38 inches)

71,1 cm (28 inches)

ball

de 7 à 7,3 cm
(from 2.8 to 2.86 inches)

seam

leather skin

wicket

bail

stump

pitch

stump

wicketkeeper

20,12 m (22 yards)

popping crease

batsman (nonstriker)

return crease

bowling crease

batsman (striker)

bowler

run

hockey

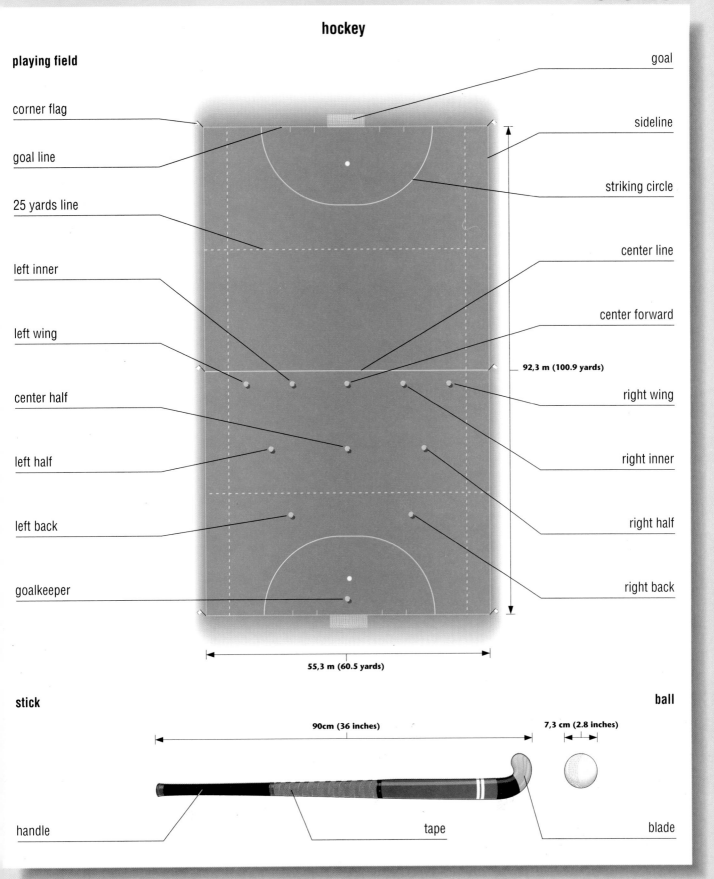

playing field

goal

corner flag

sideline

goal line

striking circle

25 yards line

center line

left inner

center forward

left wing

92,3 m (100.9 yards)

right wing

center half

right inner

left half

right half

left back

right back

goalkeeper

55,3 m (60.5 yards)

stick

ball

90cm (36 inches)

7,3 cm (2.8 inches)

handle

tape

blade

ice hockey

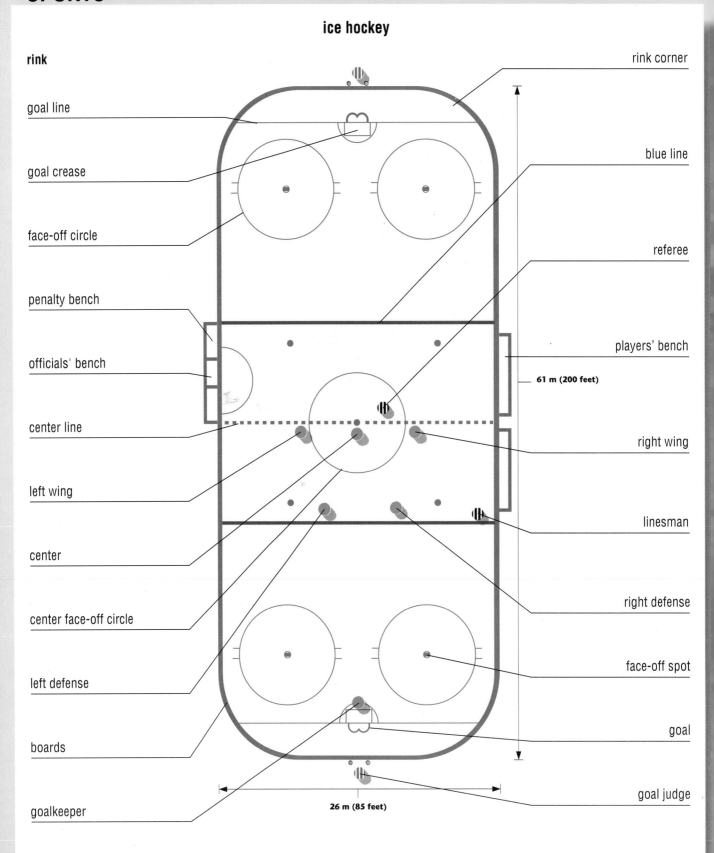

rink

goal line

goal crease

face-off circle

penalty bench

officials' bench

center line

left wing

center

center face-off circle

left defense

boards

goalkeeper

rink corner

blue line

referee

players' bench

61 m (200 feet)

right wing

linesman

right defense

face-off spot

goal

goal judge

26 m (85 feet)

ice hockey

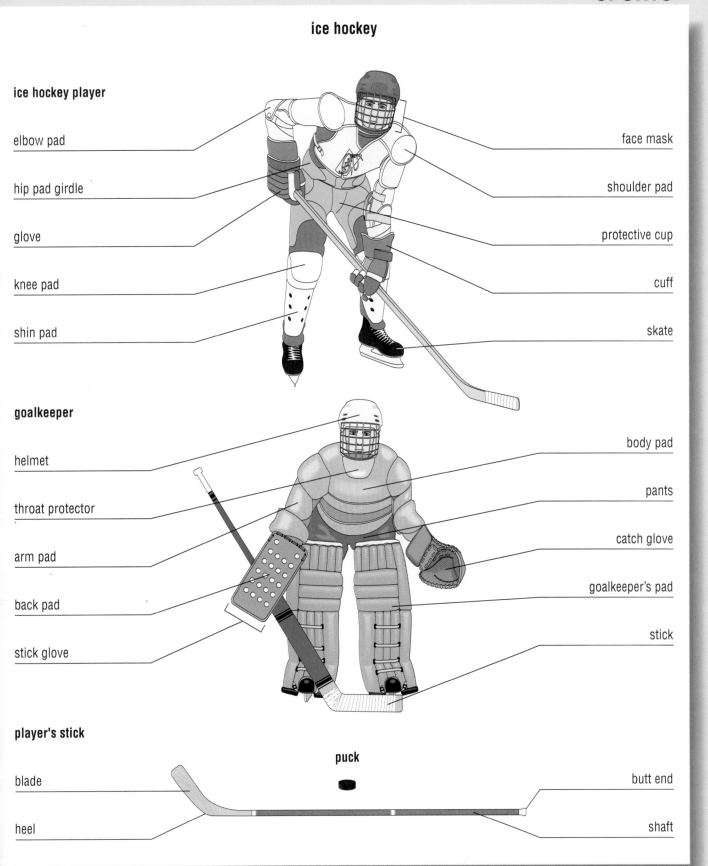

ice hockey player

elbow pad

hip pad girdle

glove

knee pad

shin pad

face mask

shoulder pad

protective cup

cuff

skate

goalkeeper

helmet

throat protector

arm pad

back pad

stick glove

body pad

pants

catch glove

goalkeeper's pad

stick

player's stick

puck

blade

heel

butt end

shaft

skating

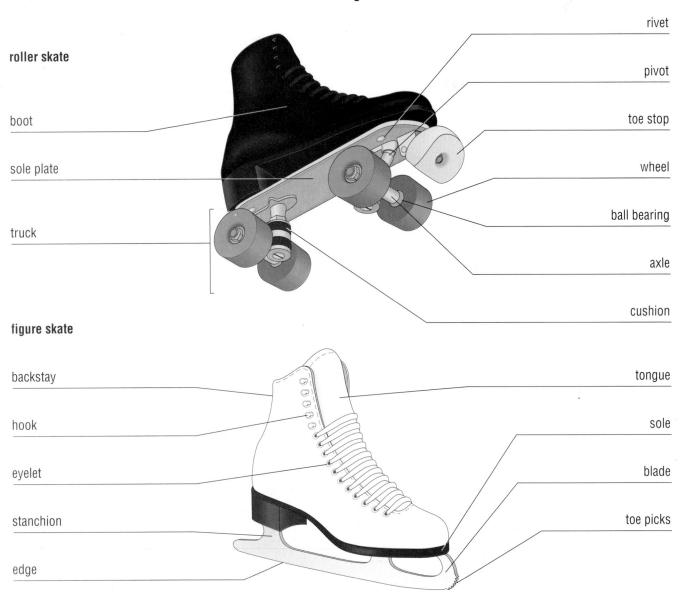

roller skate

rivet

pivot

boot

toe stop

sole plate

wheel

ball bearing

truck

axle

cushion

figure skate

backstay

tongue

hook

sole

eyelet

blade

stanchion

toe picks

edge

speed skate

hockey skate

tendon guard

toe box

point

basketball

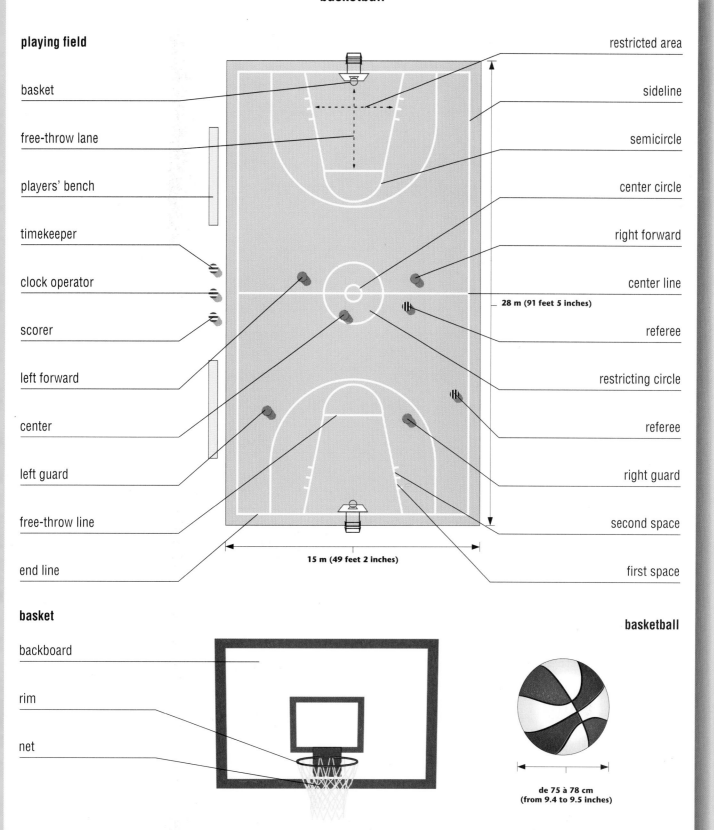

playing field

basket

free-throw lane

players' bench

timekeeper

clock operator

scorer

left forward

center

left guard

free-throw line

end line

restricted area

sideline

semicircle

center circle

right forward

center line

28 m (91 feet 5 inches)

referee

restricting circle

referee

right guard

second space

first space

15 m (49 feet 2 inches)

basket

backboard

rim

net

basketball

**de 75 à 78 cm
(from 9.4 to 9.5 inches)**

tennis

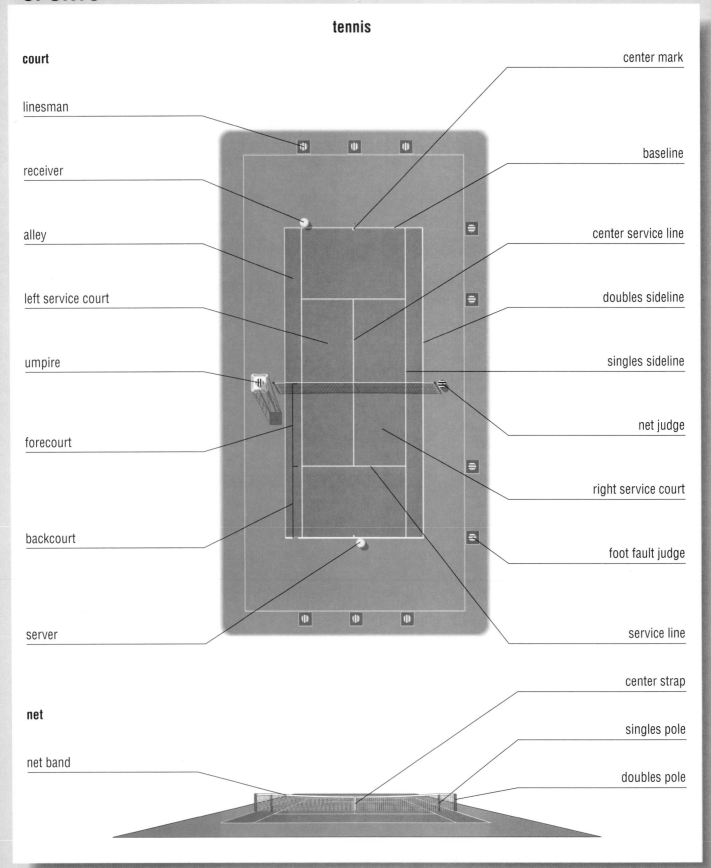

court

linesman

receiver

alley

left service court

umpire

forecourt

backcourt

server

center mark

baseline

center service line

doubles sideline

singles sideline

net judge

right service court

foot fault judge

service line

center strap

singles pole

doubles pole

net

net band

tennis

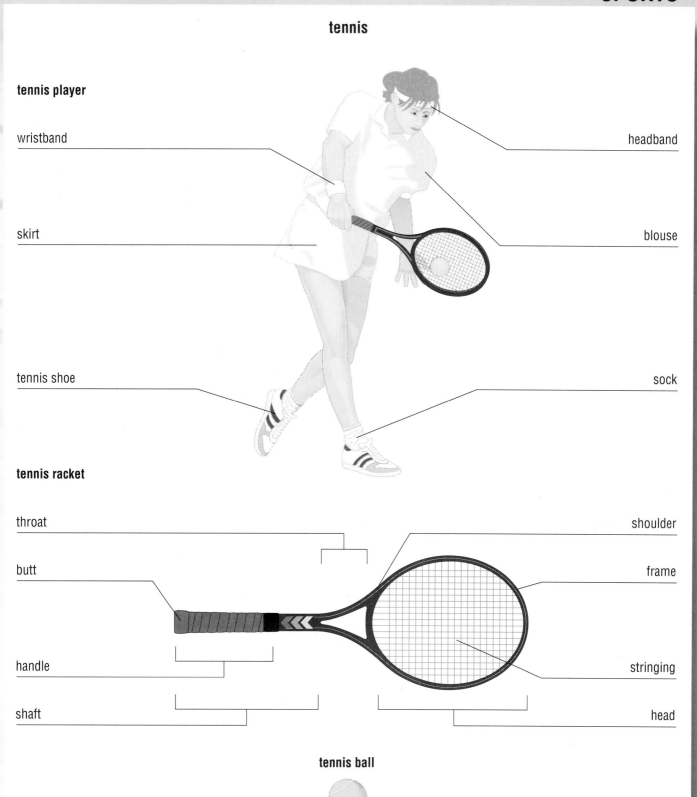

tennis player

wristband

headband

skirt

blouse

tennis shoe

sock

tennis racket

throat

shoulder

butt

frame

handle

stringing

shaft

head

tennis ball

alpine skiing

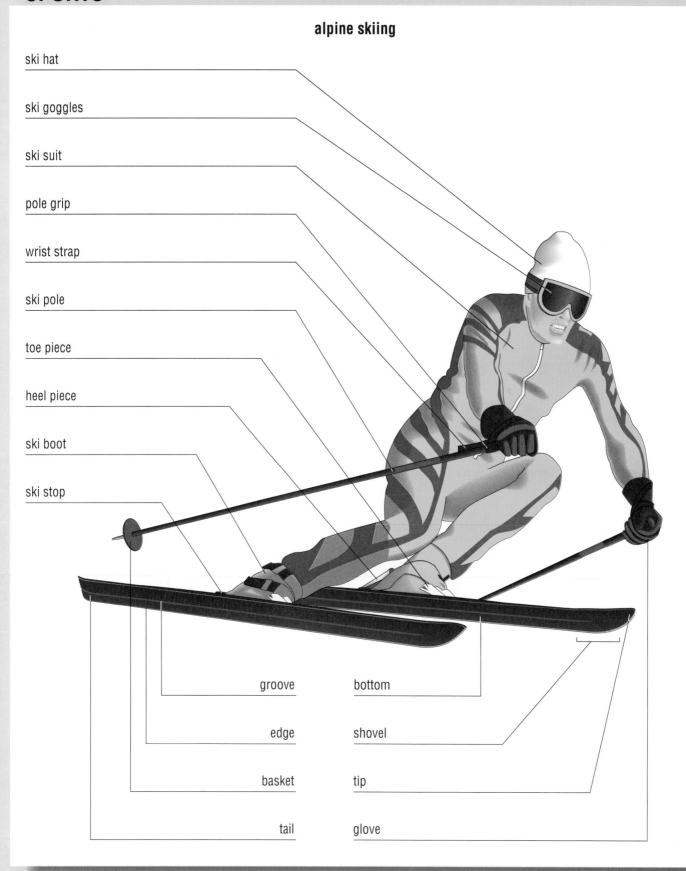

ski hat

ski goggles

ski suit

pole grip

wrist strap

ski pole

toe piece

heel piece

ski boot

ski stop

groove

bottom

edge

shovel

basket

tip

tail

glove

cross-country skiing

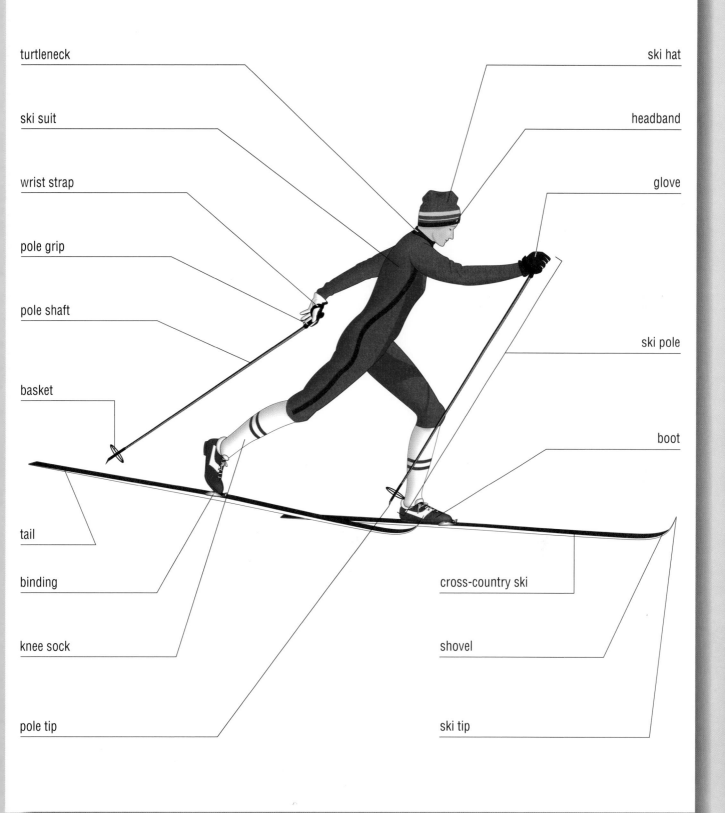

turtleneck

ski suit

wrist strap

pole grip

pole shaft

basket

tail

binding

knee sock

pole tip

ski hat

headband

glove

ski pole

boot

cross-country ski

shovel

ski tip

SPORTS

diving

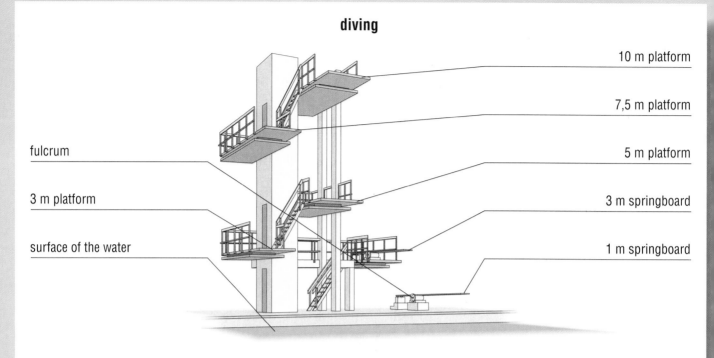

10 m platform

7,5 m platform

fulcrum

5 m platform

3 m platform

3 m springboard

surface of the water

1 m springboard

swimming

swimming pool

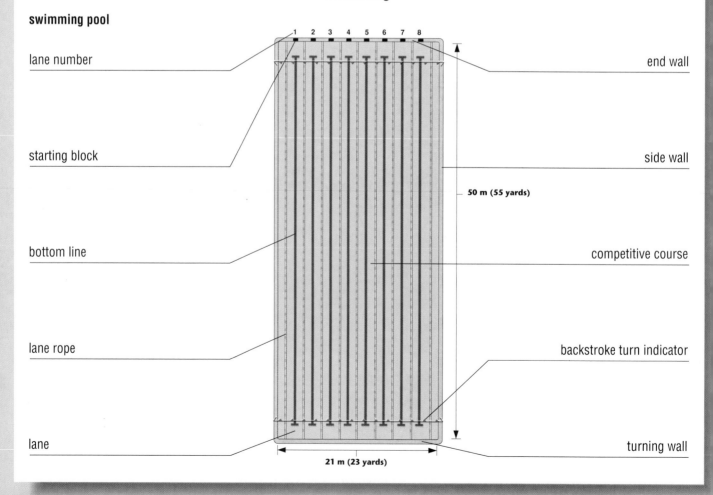

lane number

end wall

starting block

side wall

50 m (55 yards)

bottom line

competitive course

lane rope

backstroke turn indicator

lane

turning wall

21 m (23 yards)

skin diving

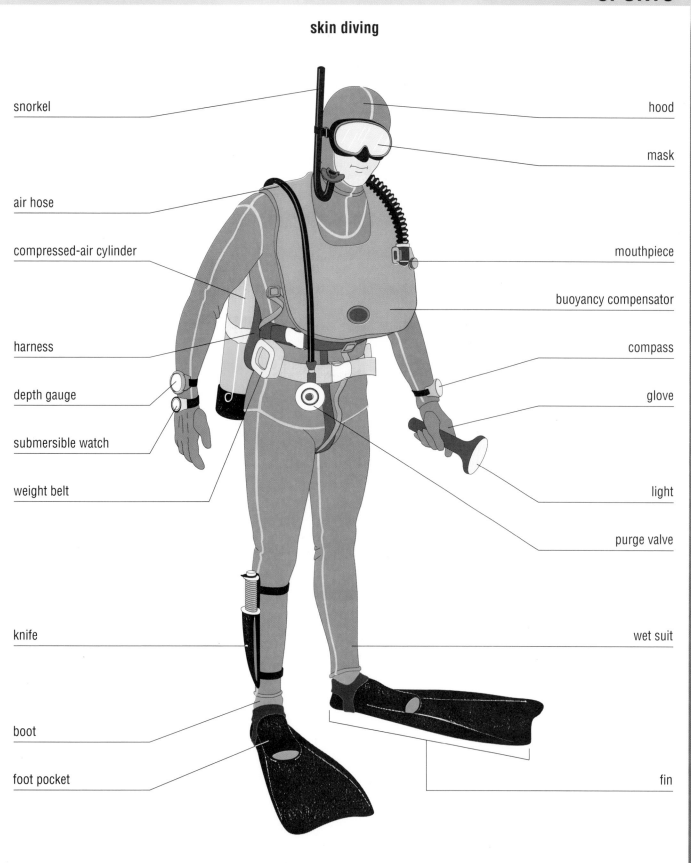

snorkel

hood

mask

air hose

compressed-air cylinder

mouthpiece

buoyancy compensator

harness

compass

depth gauge

glove

submersible watch

weight belt

light

purge valve

knife

wet suit

boot

foot pocket

fin

sailboard

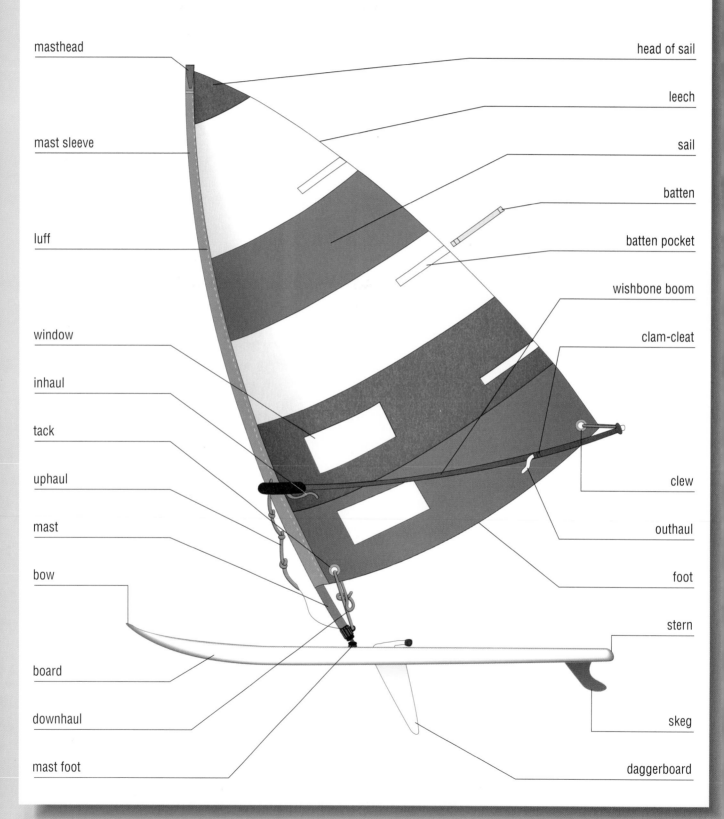

masthead

mast sleeve

luff

window

inhaul

tack

uphaul

mast

bow

board

downhaul

mast foot

head of sail

leech

sail

batten

batten pocket

wishbone boom

clam-cleat

clew

outhaul

foot

stern

skeg

daggerboard

game of darts

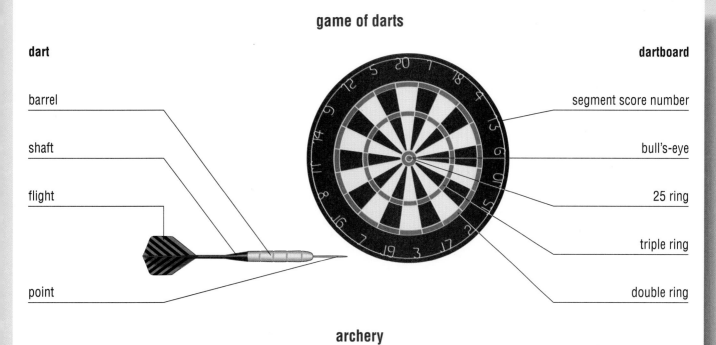

dart

barrel

shaft

flight

point

dartboard

segment score number

bull's-eye

25 ring

triple ring

double ring

archery

arrow

point

shaft

nock

feathering

nocking point

cable guard

bowstring

compound bow

cable

sight

arrow rest

grip

stabilizer

mounting bracket

limb

wheel

camping equipment

tent

door

canopy

guy line

strainer

sewn-in floor

rainfly

inner tent

elastic strainer

peg

zipper

family tent

canvas divider

living room

guy line

room

peg loop

frame

wall

elastic strainer

window canopy

screen window

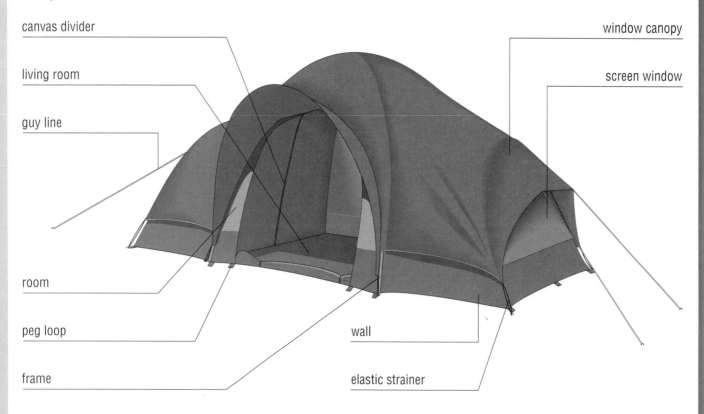

camping equipment

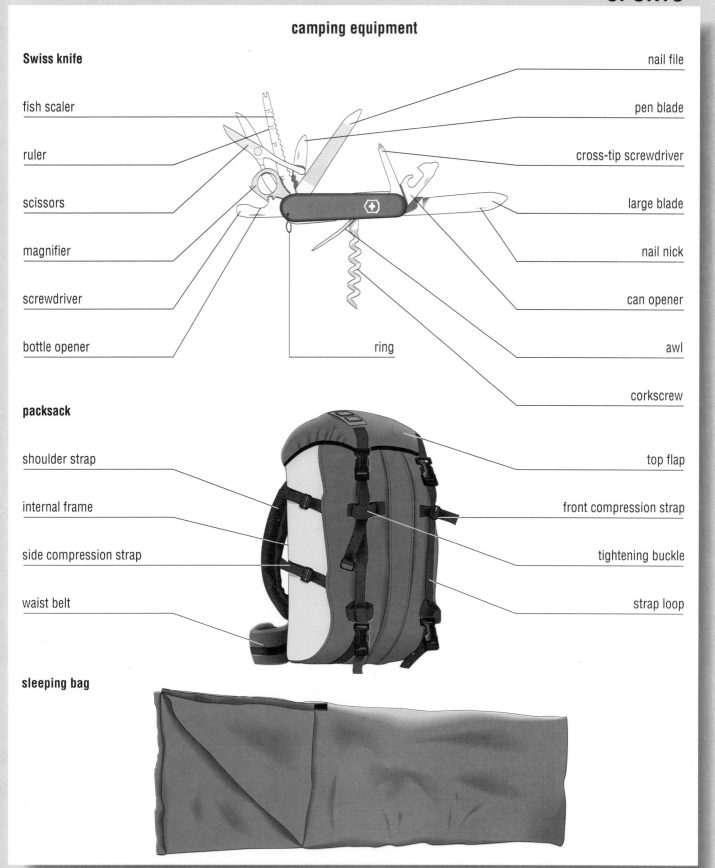

Swiss knife

nail file

fish scaler

pen blade

ruler

cross-tip screwdriver

scissors

large blade

magnifier

nail nick

screwdriver

can opener

bottle opener

ring

awl

corkscrew

packsack

shoulder strap

top flap

internal frame

front compression strap

side compression strap

tightening buckle

waist belt

strap loop

sleeping bag

indoor games

backgammon

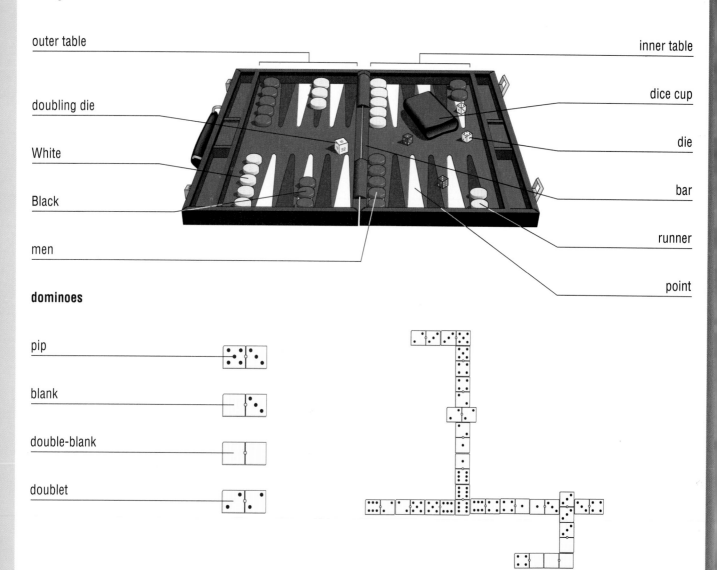

outer table

inner table

doubling die

dice cup

White

die

Black

bar

men

runner

point

dominoes

pip

blank

double-blank

doublet

card games

Joker   Ace   King   Queen   Jack   diamond   heart   spade   club

measure of time

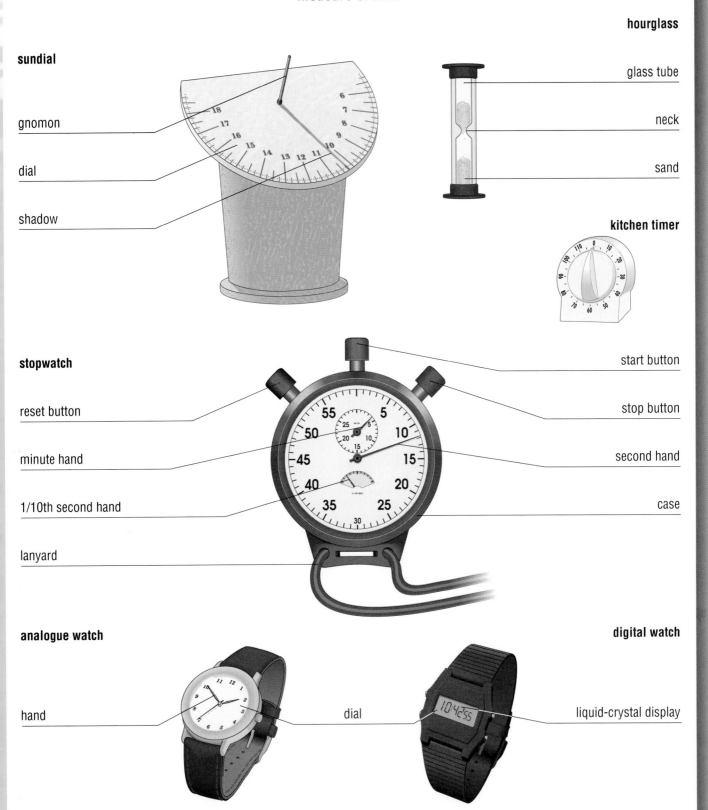

hourglass

glass tube

neck

sand

sundial

gnomon

dial

shadow

kitchen timer

stopwatch

reset button

minute hand

1/10th second hand

lanyard

start button

stop button

second hand

case

analogue watch

hand

dial

digital watch

liquid-crystal display

MEASURING DEVICES

measure of weight

Roberval's balance

dial

pointer

pan

beam

base

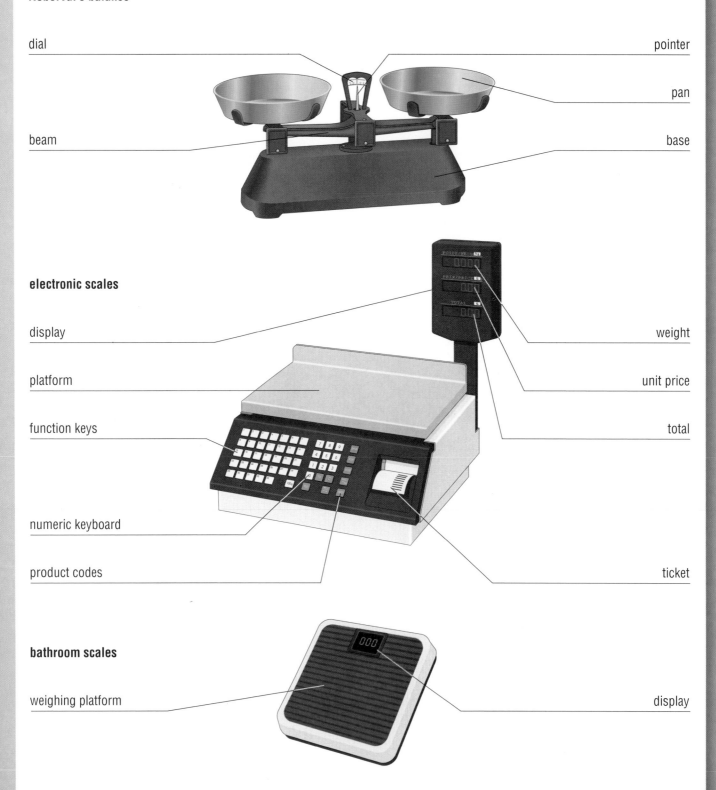

electronic scales

display

weight

platform

unit price

function keys

total

numeric keyboard

product codes

ticket

bathroom scales

weighing platform

display

measure of temperature

thermometer

Fahrenheit scale

Celsius scale

F degrees

C degrees

mercury column

bulb

clinical thermometer

expansion chamber

stem

capillary bore

scale

constriction

mercury bulb

room thermostat

desired temperature

temperature set point knob

pointer

cover

backplate

actual temperature

measure of length

tape measure

case

tape lock

tape

hook

measure of distance

pedometer

clip

step setting

pointer

OPTICAL INSTRUMENTS

binoculars

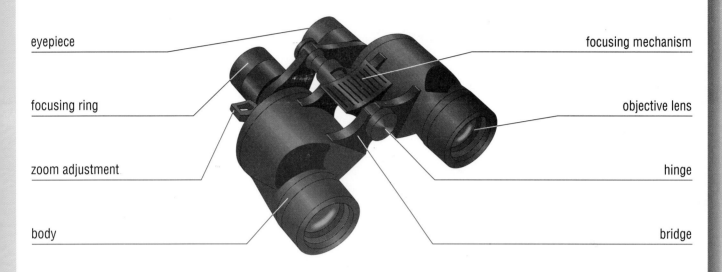

eyepiece

focusing ring

zoom adjustment

body

focusing mechanism

objective lens

hinge

bridge

binocular microscope

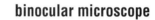
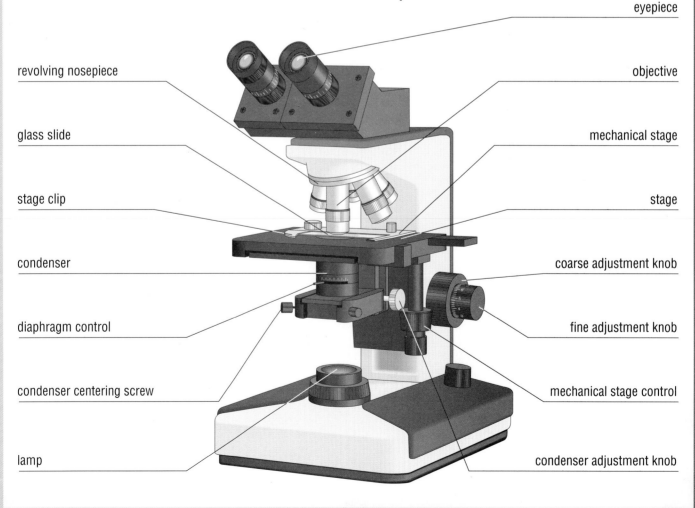

revolving nosepiece

glass slide

stage clip

condenser

diaphragm control

condenser centering screw

lamp

eyepiece

objective

mechanical stage

stage

coarse adjustment knob

fine adjustment knob

mechanical stage control

condenser adjustment knob

reflecting telescope

finder

focusing knob

support

eyepiece

azimut clamp

main tube

altitude clamp

cradle

eyepiece

light

flat mirror

main mirror

refracting telescope

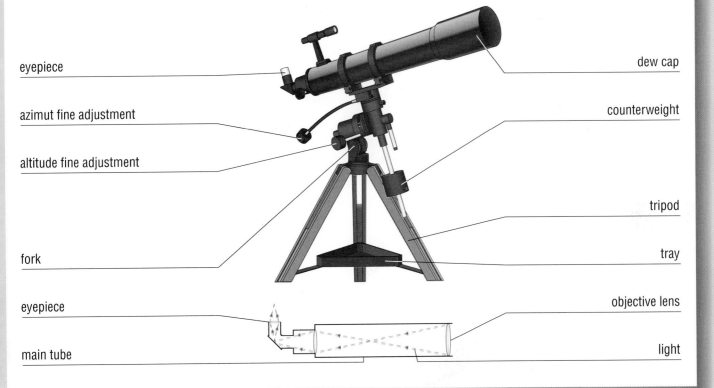

eyepiece

dew cap

azimut fine adjustment

counterweight

altitude fine adjustment

tripod

fork

tray

eyepiece

objective lens

main tube

light

fire engines

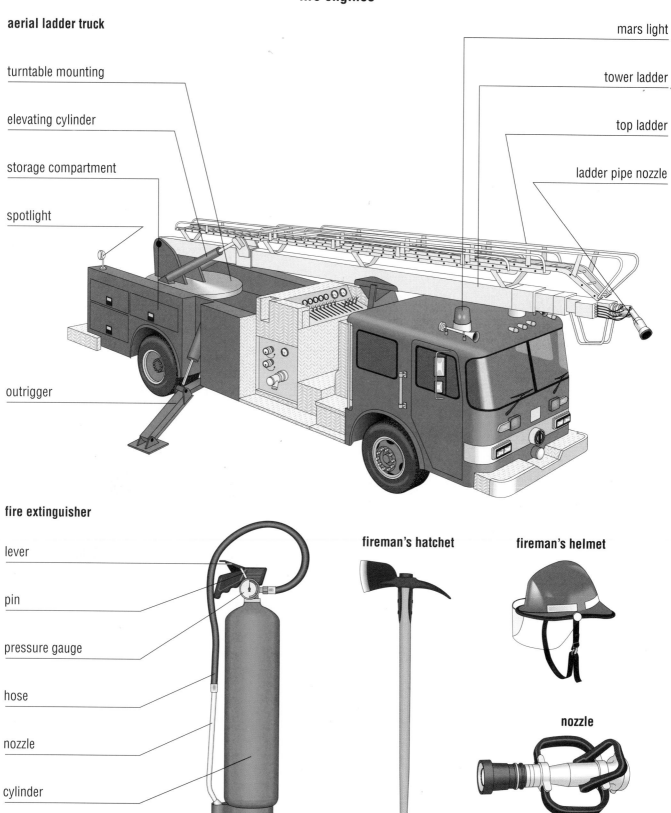

aerial ladder truck

turntable mounting

elevating cylinder

storage compartment

spotlight

outrigger

mars light

tower ladder

top ladder

ladder pipe nozzle

fire extinguisher

lever

pin

pressure gauge

hose

nozzle

cylinder

fireman's hatchet

fireman's helmet

nozzle

fire engines

pumper

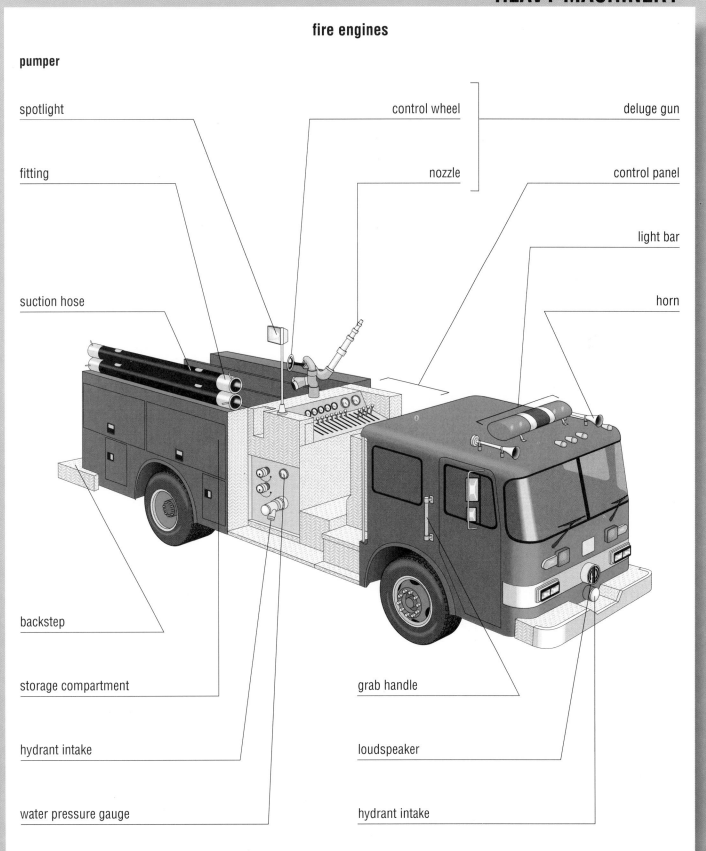

spotlight

control wheel

deluge gun

fitting

nozzle

control panel

light bar

horn

suction hose

backstep

storage compartment

grab handle

hydrant intake

loudspeaker

water pressure gauge

hydrant intake

HEAVY MACHINERY

material handling

tower crane

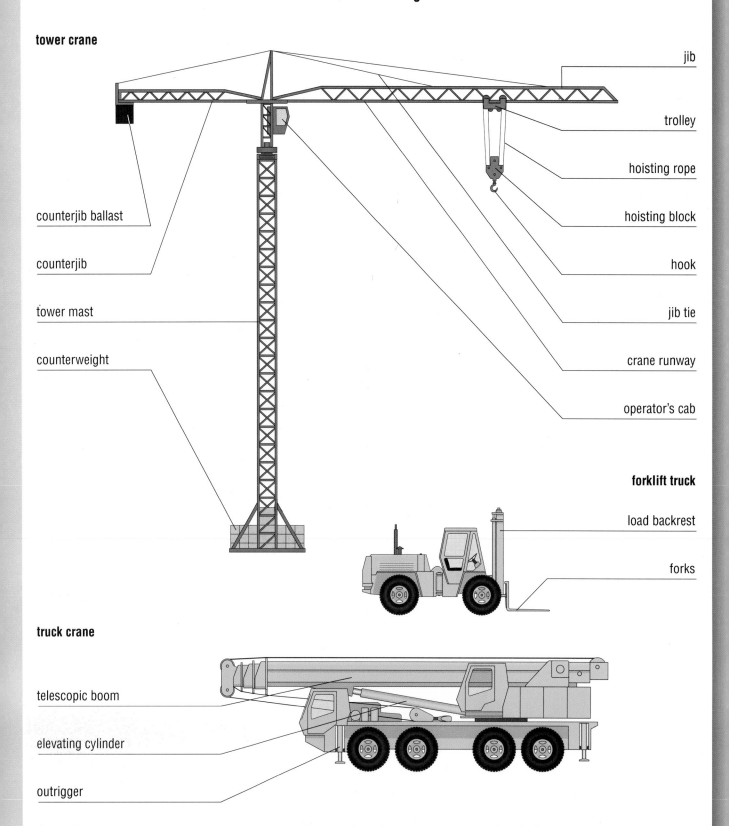

jib

trolley

hoisting rope

hoisting block

hook

jib tie

crane runway

operator's cab

counterjib ballast

counterjib

tower mast

counterweight

forklift truck

load backrest

forks

truck crane

telescopic boom

elevating cylinder

outrigger

bulldozer

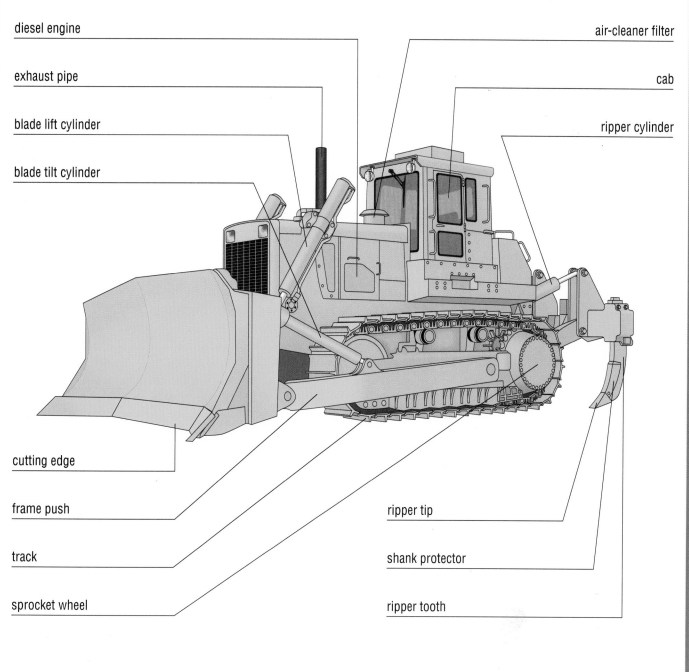

diesel engine

exhaust pipe

blade lift cylinder

blade tilt cylinder

air-cleaner filter

cab

ripper cylinder

cutting edge

frame push

track

sprocket wheel

ripper tip

shank protector

ripper tooth

blade

crawer tractor

ripper

wheel loader

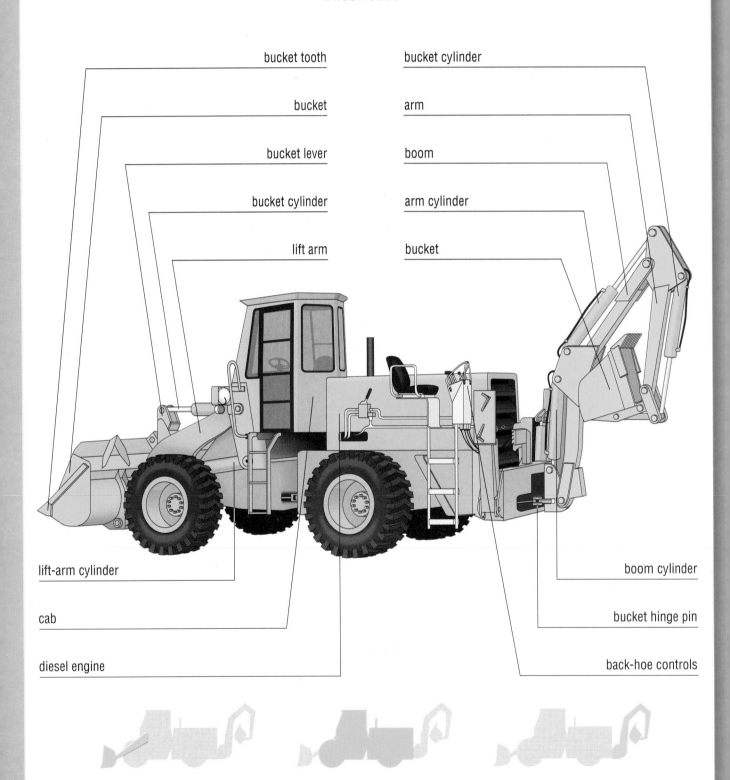

bucket tooth

bucket cylinder

bucket

arm

bucket lever

boom

bucket cylinder

arm cylinder

lift arm

bucket

lift-arm cylinder

boom cylinder

cab

bucket hinge pin

diesel engine

back-hoe controls

front-end loader

tractor

back-hoe

dump truck

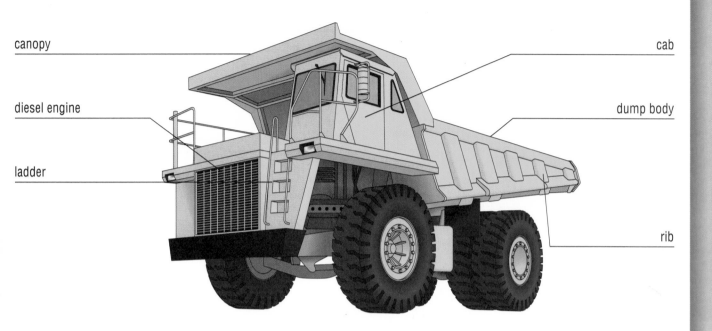

canopy

cab

diesel engine

dump body

ladder

rib

hydraulic shovel

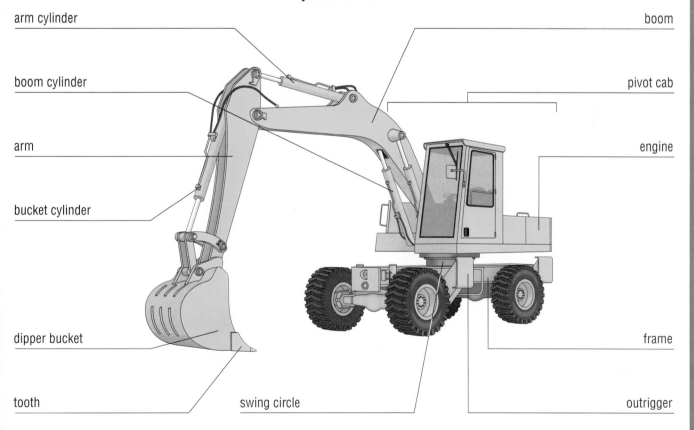

arm cylinder

boom

boom cylinder

pivot cab

arm

engine

bucket cylinder

dipper bucket

frame

tooth

swing circle

outrigger

SYMBOLS

public signs

telephone

informations

handicapped

no smoking

toilets

service station

restaurant

hospital

poison

flammable

explosive

electrical hazard

major road signs

speed limit

no parking

no entry

stop

one-way traffic

bicycle lane

right turn

yield

school

traffic lights

danger

pedestrian crossing

1 m springboard 134.
1/10th second hand 141.
10 m platform 134.
10 yards line 119.
1st valve slide 115.
25 ring 137.
25 yards line 119, 125.
2nd valve slide 115.
3 m platform 134.
3 m springboard 134.
3rd valve slide 115.
5 m platform 134.
5 yards line 119.
7,5 m platform 134.

A
a 112.
abdomen 24, 25, 26, 31.
abdominal segment 24.
abutment 97.
acanthus leaf 61.
accessory shoe 87, 89.
accidentals 112.
Ace 140.
action assembly 113.
actual temperature 143.
add in memory 74.
add key 74.
adhesive tape 72.
adjustable wrench 76.
adjusting screw 76.
aerial ladder truck 146.
Africa 12.
air hose 135.
air inlet 105.
air lock 103.
air unit 78.
air-cleaner filter 149.
ala 36.
alighting board 25.
alley 130.
almond 46.
alpine skiing 132.
alternator warning light 91.
altitude clamp 145.
altitude fine adjustment 145.
AM-FM cassette player 86.
AM-FM cassette recorder 86.
AM-FM tuner 86, 89.
American corn bread 37.
American white bread 37.
ammunition stowage 111.
amplifier 89.
anal fin 27.
analogue watch 141.
anchor 102.
ankle 31.
announcement time selector 85.
annual ring 18.
Antarctica 12.
antenna 24, 25, 26, 86, 90, 104, 111.
antennule 26.
anther 17.
anti-slip shoe 77.
anti-torque tail rotor 105.
anticollision light 104.
apple 43.
apricot 43.
apron 60, 61.
aquatic bird 23.
aquatic bird 23.
arbor 51.
arch 97.
arch bridge 97.
archery 137.
Arctic 12.
arm 20, 32, 53, 150, 151.
arm cylinder 150, 151.
arm guard 121.
arm pad 127.
arm stump 61.
armchair 61.
armor 108.
armor 111.
armored plate 111.
armrest 61.
arrow 137.
arrow rest 137.

artichoke 41.
articulated road train 94.
ash layer 13.
Asia 12.
asparagus 39.
assist handle 93.
asteroids 9.
Atlantic Ocean 12.
audio system 91.
auricle 35.
Australia 12.
auto dialer index 85.
auto reverse 86.
auto-off switch 53.
autofocus on/off switch 87.
automatic drip coffee maker 68.
automobile 90, 91.
automobile car 101.
autumn squash 42.
auxiliary handle 76.
avocado 45.
awl 139.
awning channel 93.
axillary bud 16.
axle 128.
azimut clamp 145.
azimut fine adjustment 145.

B
b 112.
back 20, 21, 22, 32, 60, 65, 75.
back judge 120.
back pad 127.
back-hoe 150.
back-hoe controls 150.
backboard 129.
backcourt 130.
backgammon 140.
backguard 69.
backstay 128.
backstep 147.
backstroke turn indicator 134.
backup light 92.
baggage compartment 100, 105.
baguette 37.
bail 124.
bailey 55.
ball bearing 72, 128.
ball, (rugby) 119.
ball, baseball 123.
ball, cricket 124.
ball, hockey 125.
ball, soccer 118.
ball, tennis 131.
ballast 100.
ballpoint pen 72.
ballroom 102.
baluster 58.
banana 45.
bar 140.
bar line 112.
barn 49.
barrel 110, 137.
base 142.
baseball 122, 123.
baseball, ball 123.
baseboard 58.
baseline 130.
basement 56.
basement window 56.
basket 129.
basket 67, 68, 129, 132, 133.
basketball 129.
basketball, field 129.
basketball, game 129.
bass clarinet 117.
bass drum 116.
bass drum 117.
bass pickup 116.
bassoon 117.
bat, baseball 123.
bat, cricket 124.
bathroom 59.
bathroom scales 142.
bathtub 59.
batrachian 27.
batsman 124.
batten 136.

batten pocket 136.
batter 123.
batter 122.
batter head 116.
batter's helmet 123.
battery 91.
batting glove 123.
battlement 55.
bay window 56.
bayonet 109.
bayonet base 63.
beach 13.
beam 142.
bean sprouts 39.
beater 68.
beater ejector 68.
beaver 108.
bed 62.
beet 40.
bell 115.
bell brace 115.
belly 20, 22.
belt 79, 83.
belt buckle 79.
belt loop 80.
Bermuda shorts 83.
berries 44.
bib 83.
bicycle 98, 99.
bicycle bag 99.
bicycle lane 152.
bidet 59.
bill 22.
bill compartment 84.
bills, major types of 23.
binding 79, 133.
binocular microscope 144.
binoculars 144.
bird 22.
bird of prey 23.
bird of prey 23.
Black 140.
black currant 44.
black rye bread 37.
black salsify 40.
Black Sea 12.
blade 149.
blade 17, 65, 75, 125, 127, 128.
blade lift cylinder 149.
blade tilt cylinder 149.
blank 140.
blanket 62.
blender 68.
blouse 131.
blouses 82.
blue 71.
blue cheese 47.
blue line 126.
blueberry 44.
board 136.
boarding step 105.
boards 126.
boat-shape pastry 48.
bodies, types of 92.
body 90.
body 93, 96, 114, 115, 144.
body flap 107.
body guard molding 93.
body pad 127.
body suit 82.
body, front view 31.
body, rear view 32.
boiler 103.
bolster 62, 65.
bolt 76.
bolt 109.
boom 150, 151.
boom cylinder 150, 151.
boot 128, 133, 135.
bottle opener 66, 139.
bottom 132.
bottom bracket axle 99.
bottom line 134.
bottom rail 57.
bow 114.
bow 102, 109, 136.
bow deck 102.

bow thruster 102.
bow window 56.
bowl 65.
bowler 124.
bowling crease 124.
bowstring 109, 137.
box spring 62.
boxcar 101.
brace 77.
brake cable 98.
brake lever 98.
brake pedal 91.
branch 18, 39.
branches 18.
Brazil nut 46.
bread 37.
bread and butter plate 64.
bread guide 68.
breast 22, 31.
breast pocket 83.
breast welt pocket 80.
breastbone 33.
breastplate 108.
bridge 84, 103, 113, 114, 144.
bridge assembly 116.
bridges 97.
brim 79.
bristles 77.
broad beans 39.
broad welt side pocket 79.
broad-leaved endive 38.
broccoli 41.
brood chamber 25.
brush 77.
brush 73.
Brussels sprouts 38.
bucket 150.
bucket cylinder 150, 151.
bucket hinge pin 150.
bucket lever 150.
bucket tooth 150.
buckle 83.
bud 17.
bulb 39, 63, 143.
bulb vegetables 41.
bulkhead flat car 101.
bull's-eye 137.
bulldozer 149.
bumper 90.
bundle 39.
bunk 103.
bunker silo 49.
buoyancy compensator 135.
bush 51.
butt 110, 131.
butt end 127.
butter compartment 70.
butter dish 64.
butterfly 24.
buttock 32.
buttoned placket 83.
buttonhole 81.

C
c 112.
c clef 112.
C degrees 143.
C-clamp 76.
cab 149, 150, 151.
cabbage lettuce 38.
cabin 105.
cabinet 88.
cable 76, 86, 137.
cable guard 137.
cable sleeve 76.
caboose 101.
cabriole 61.
cake 48.
calf 32, 50.
caliper 95.
Callisto 9.
calls indicator 85.
calyx 17.
cambium 18.
camel 30.
Camembert 47.
camera 87.
camera body 87.

The terms in **bold type** indicate the title of an illustration.

153

camping equipment 138, 139.
can opener 66, 139.
canine 34.
cannon 20, 111.
canopy 84, 138, 151.
cantaloupe 42.
cantilever bridge 97.
cantilever span 97.
canvas divider 138.
cap 79.
cap 19, 72.
capillary bore 143.
captain's quarters 102.
car coat 82.
car wash 96.
carafe 68.
carapace 26, 28.
caravan 93.
caraway seeded rye bread 37.
card games 140.
card slot 84.
cardigan 81.
cardoon 39.
Caribbean Sea 12.
carpal bone 33.
carpentry 75.
carrier 98.
carrot 40.
cars, types of 101.
cartridge 72, 110.
case 113, 141, 143.
cash readout 96.
cashew 46.
cassette 86.
cassette deck 89.
cassette holder 89.
cassette loading slot 88.
cassette player 86.
cassette player controls 86.
castanets 117.
castle 55.
castle 55.
cat 21.
cat's forepaw 21.
cat's head 21.
catch glove 127.
catcher 123.
catcher 122.
catcher's glove 123.
catenary 100.
caterpillar 24.
cauliflower 41.
cave 14.
cave 13.
CD player 89.
ceiling fixture 63.
celeriac 40.
celery 39.
cell 25.
cello 117.
Celsius scale 143.
center 120, 126, 129.
center back 118.
center circle 118, 129.
center console 91.
center face-off circle 126.
center field 122.
center fielder 122.
center flag 118.
center forward 118, 125.
center half 125.
center line 125, 126, 129.
center mark 130.
center service line 130.
center span 97.
center spot 118.
center strap 130.
Central America 12.
central processing unit 74.
cephalothorax 26.
chain 99.
chain guide 99.
chain mail 108.
chain stay 98.
chain wheels 99.
chandelier 63.
channel scan buttons 88.

channel selector control 88.
chapel 55.
charlotte 48.
cheek 21, 31, 75.
cheeses 47.
cherimoya 45.
cherry 43.
chest 20, 31.
chest protector 121, 123.
chestnut 20, 46.
Chèvre 47.
chick 50.
chick-peas 39.
chicory 38.
children's clothing 83.
chimney 56.
chimney pot 56.
chimney stack 56.
chin 22, 31.
chin strap 121.
China Sea 12.
Chinese cabbage 38.
chive 41.
chrysalis 24.
chuck 76.
circle 71.
citrus fruits 44.
citrus juicer 66.
clam-cleat 136.
clarinet 117.
classic blouse 82.
classical guitar 114.
claw 21, 22, 24, 26, 28, 75.
claw hammer 75.
clear key 74.
clear-entry key 74.
cleated shoe 121.
clefs 112.
clew 136.
cliff 13, 14.
climbing plant 51.
clinical thermometer 143.
clip 73.
clip 72, 143.
clock 91.
clock operator 129.
clock timer 69.
cloud 15.
cloud of volcanic ash 13.
club 140.
club chair 61.
clump of flowers 51.
clutch lever 95.
clutch pedal 91.
coach car 100.
coach's box 122.
coarse adjustment knob 144.
coastal features 13.
coats 82.
cob 39.
cobbler 48.
cockleshell 61.
coconut 46.
coffee mug 64.
coin pocket 84.
coin purse 84.
coin return bucket 85.
coin return knob 85.
coin slot 85.
coinbox telephone 85.
colander 66.
collar 16, 78.
collarbone 33.
column 14.
coma 11.
comet 11.
comforter 62.
command control dial 87.
command module 106.
commander's seat 111.
commando knife 109.
commissure of lips 34.
compass 135.
compass bridge 102.
competitive course 134.
compound bow 137.
compound eye 24, 25.

compressed-air cylinder 135.
condenser 144.
condenser adjustment knob 144.
condenser centering screw 144.
conductor's podium 117.
cone 13, 71.
conning tower 103.
constellations 11.
constriction 143.
container 68.
container car 101.
continents 12.
contrabassoon 117.
control cable 99.
control deck 103.
control knob 69.
control panel 87, 147.
control stick 105.
control wheel 147.
convection zone 10.
convertible 92.
cooking utensils 67.
cooktop 69.
cooktop edge 69.
cordless telephone 85.
core 10.
corkscrew 66, 139.
corn 39.
corn salad 38.
corner arc 118.
corner flag 118, 125.
corner tower 55.
cornet 117.
cornice 56, 57.
corolla 17.
corona 10.
cos lettuce 38.
Cottage cheese 47.
counter 78.
counterjib 148.
counterjib ballast 148.
counterweight 145, 148.
coupler head 100.
court 130.
couter 108.
cover 123, 143.
covered parapet walk 55.
cow 50.
cowshed 49.
cradle 145.
crak rye bread 37.
cranberry 44.
crane runway 148.
crank 99, 109.
crater 13.
crawer tractor 149.
cream puff 48.
creamer 64.
crease 80.
crème caramel 48.
crenel 55.
crêpe Suzette 48.
crest 14.
crew neck sweater 81.
cricket 124.
cricket, ball 124.
crisper 70.
crocodile 29.
croissant 37.
crook 115.
cross rail 60.
cross-country ski 133.
cross-country skiing 133.
cross-tip screwdriver 139.
crossbar 98.
crossbow 109.
crosspiece 60.
croup 20.
crown 18, 22, 79.
crustacean 26.
cube 71.
cucumber 42.
cuff 80, 127.
cuisse 108.
culotte 82.
cup 64.
curled endive 38.

curled kale 38.
currant 44.
curtain wall 55.
curved jaw 76.
cushion 128.
cutting blade 68.
cutting edge 65, 149.
cutting weapons 109.
cylinder 71, 110, 146.
cymbals 117.

d 112.
daggerboard 136.
dairy 49.
dairy compartment 70.
damper pedal 113.
dandelion 38.
danger 152.
Danish Blue 47.
Danish rye bread 37.
dart 137.
dart 83.
dartboard 137.
darts, game 137.
dashboard 91.
dashboard 95.
data display 89.
date 43.
dead ball line 119.
deadly poisonous mushroom 19.
decimal key 74.
deck 97.
deep fryer 67.
defensive 120.
Deimos 9.
deluge gun 147.
demitasse 64.
depressed-center flat car 101.
depth gauge 135.
desired temperature 143.
desserts 48.
destroying angel 19.
dew 15.
dew cap 145.
dewclaw 21.
dial 141, 142.
diamond 140.
diaphragm 89.
diaphragm control 144.
dice cup 140.
die 140.
diesel engine 149, 150, 151.
diesel-electric locomotive 100.
digital watch 141.
dining room 102.
dinner plate 64.
dinnerware 64.
dipper bucket 151.
disk brake 95.
disk drive 74.
dispenser 72.
display 74, 142.
display panel 88.
distance, measure of 143.
divide key 74.
diving 134.
dog 21.
domestic appliances 68.
dominoes 140.
door 70, 90, 93, 104, 138.
door handle 90.
door lock 90.
door mirror 94.
door open warning light 91.
door shelf 70.
doorknob 57.
dormant volcano 13.
dorsum 36.
double bass 117.
double boiler 67.
double ring 137.
double-blank 140.
double-breasted buttoning 79.
doubles pole 130.
doubles sideline 130.
doublet 140.
doubling die 140.

The terms in **bold type** indicate the title of an illustration.

doughnut 48.
downhaul 136.
downspout 56.
draining spoon 66.
drawbridge 55.
drawer 60, 69.
drawstring 84.
drive chain 98.
drive shaft 105.
driver's cab 100.
driver's seat 111.
drop leaf 60.
drums 116.
dry gallery 14.
dual seat 95.
duck 50.
dump body 151.
dump truck 151.
dune 13.
dust tail 11.
Dutch oven 67.

e 112.
ear 35, 60.
ear canal 35.
eardrum 27, 28.
earphone 86.
Earth 9.
edge 128, 132.
edging 51.
edible mushroom 19.
egg tray 70.
eggplant 42.
eighth note 112.
eighth rest 112.
eject 88.
elastic strainer 138.
elastic waistband 80.
elbow 20, 21, 32.
elbow pad 121, 127.
electric drill 76.
electric guitar 116.
electric range 69.
electrical hazard 152.
electrified fence 49.
electronic flash 87.
electronic scales 142.
electronic viewfinder 89.
electronic viewfinder controls 89.
elephant 29.
elevating cylinder 146, 148.
elevator 104.
elevon 107.
Emmenthal 47.
end button 114.
end line 129.
end wall 134.
end zone 120.
engine 111, 151.
engine room 102, 103.
engines 107.
English horn 117.
English loaf 37.
entrance 25.
entrance slide 25.
epaulet 79.
equal key 74.
equipment 52, 53.
eraser 72.
eraser 72.
eraser holder 72.
Europa 9.
Europe 12.
excretory opening 26.
exhaust pipe 95, 105, 149.
exhaust stack 94.
exit cone 25.
expansion chamber 143.
explosive 152.
exposure mode 87.
extension ladder 77.
exterior door 57.
eye 22, 26, 28, 35, 75.
eyeball 27.
eyebrow 35.
eyecup 89.

eyelash 35.
eyelet 78, 84, 128.
eyelet tab 78.
eyelid 28.
eyepiece 144, 145.

f 112.
f clef 112.
F degrees 143.
F-1 engine 106.
face 31, 75.
face mask 121, 127.
face-off circle 126.
face-off spot 126.
faculae 10.
Fahrenheit scale 143.
fairing 95.
fallow 49.
family tent 138.
fan trellis 51.
farm's animals 50.
farmhouse 49.
farmhouse bread 37.
farmstead 49.
farmyard 49.
fast forward 88.
fast-forward button 86.
fauces 34.
faucet 59.
fauld 108.
feather 22.
feathering 137.
feet, major types of 23.
felt hat 79.
fender 90, 95, 98.
fennel 39.
ferrule 65, 77.
fetlock 20.
fibula 33.
fifth wheel 94.
figure skate 128.
filament 10, 17, 63.
filler hole 94.
film advance mode 87.
film rewind 87.
film speed 87.
filter 67.
fin 105, 135.
finder 145.
fine adjustment knob 144.
finger 21, 27, 123.
fingerboard 114.
fingernail 36.
fire engines 146, 147.
fire extinguisher 146.
fireman's hatchet 146.
fireman's helmet 146.
first base 122.
first baseman 122.
first dorsal fin 27.
first floor 56.
first quarter 10.
first space 129.
first stage 106.
first violin 117.
first-class cabin 104.
fish 27.
fish platter 64.
fish scaler 139.
fitted sheet 62.
fitting 147.
fixed jaw 76.
flagstone 51.
flammable 152.
flank 20, 22.
flank forward 119.
flanking tower 55.
flap 84.
flap pocket 80.
flare 10.
flashtube 87.
flat 112.
flat car 101.
flat mirror 145.
flat sheet 62.
flews 21.
flight 137.

flight deck 104, 105, 107.
floor lamp 63.
floppydisk 74.
flower 16.
flower bed 51.
flower bud 16.
flower, parts of a 17.
flush handle 59.
flute 117.
fly 80, 83.
fly agaric 19.
fob pocket 83.
focusing knob 145.
focusing mechanism 144.
focusing ring 87, 144.
fodder corn 49.
fog 15.
fog light 92.
folding door 59.
foliage 18.
foot 22, 26, 32, 136.
foot fault judge 130.
foot pocket 135.
foot-jaws 26.
football 121.
football, equipment 121.
football, game 120, 121.
football, uniform 121.
footboard 62.
footbridge 55.
footrest 95.
forearm 21, 32.
forecourt 130.
forehead 22, 31.
foreleg 24, 25.
forest 14.
forewing 24, 25.
fork 65.
fork 98, 145.
forklift truck 148.
forks 148.
forward slide change 87.
foul line 122.
fountain pen 72.
four-door sedan 92.
fourchette 79.
frame 25, 76, 95, 131, 138, 151.
frame push 149.
free-throw lane 129.
free-throw line 129.
freewheel 99.
freezer compartment 70.
freight hold 104.
French bread 37.
French horn 117.
fret 114, 116.
frog 27, 114.
front brake 98.
front compression strap 139.
front derailleur 98, 99.
front headlights 92.
front leg 60.
front pocket 84.
front sight 110.
front top pocket 80, 83.
front-end loader 150.
fruit 16.
fruit salad 48.
fruit vegetables 42.
frying pan 67.
fuel indicator 91.
fuel tank 94, 95, 100, 105, 111.
fulcrum 134.
full back 119.
full moon 10.
fullback 120.
fumarole 13.
fume extractor 111.
function keys 142.
funnel 66, 102.
fuselage 104.

g 112.
g clef 112.
gable 56.
gable vent 56.
galaxy 11.

galley 104.
Ganymede 9.
garage 56.
garage driveway 56.
garden fork 52.
garden hose 53.
garden sorrel 38.
garlic 41.
gas pedal 91.
gas tail 11.
gas tank door 90.
gaskin 20.
gasoline pump 96.
gasoline pump 96.
gasoline pump hose 96.
gastropod 26.
gate leg 60.
gate-leg table 60.
gauntlet 108.
gearshift lever 91, 95.
generator 98.
genital opening 26.
German rye bread 37.
geyser 13.
gibbous moon 10.
gill 19.
gill cover 27.
giraffe 29.
glass cover 70.
glass slide 144.
glass tube 141.
glottis 28.
glove 123.
glove 127, 132, 133, 135.
glove compartment 91.
glove finger 79.
gloves 79.
glue stick 73.
gnomon 141.
goal 118, 119, 120, 125, 126.
goal area 118.
goal crease 126.
goal judge 126.
goal line 118, 119, 120, 125, 126.
goalkeeper 127.
goalkeeper 118, 125, 126.
goalkeeper's pad 127.
goat 50.
gondola car 101.
gong 117.
goose 50.
gooseberry 44.
gorge 14.
Gorgonzola 47.
grab handle 94, 147.
granulation 10.
grape 44.
grapefruit 44.
graphic equalizer 89.
grass bag 53.
grater 66.
gravy boat 64.
greave 108.
Greek bread 37.
green 71.
green bean 42.
green cabbage 38.
green peas 39.
greenhouse 49.
grille 90.
grip 137.
groin 31.
groove 109, 132.
Gruyère 47.
guard 58.
guard rail 70.
guardhouse 55.
guava 45.
gun flap 79.
gunner's sight 111.
gusset 84.
gutter 56.
guy line 138.

The terms in **bold type** indicate the title of an illustration.

INDEX

H

hail 15.
hailstone 15.
hair 32, 114.
half note 112.
half rest 112.
halfway line 118, 119.
hammer 75.
hammer 110, 113.
hammer rail 113.
hand 32, 36, 141.
hand cultivator 52.
hand fork 52.
hand trowel 52.
hand warmer pocket 80.
hand weeder 52.
handbag 84.
handgrip 95.
handicapped 152.
handkerchief 83.
handle 53, 65, 68, 69, 70, 75, 76, 77, 84, 86, 114, 123, 124, 125, 131.
handlebars 98.
handrail 58.
handsaw 75.
handset 85.
handset cord 85.
hanger loop 81.
hanging basket 51.
hanging pendant 63.
hard cheese 47.
hard palate 34.
harness 135.
harp 117.
hatband 79.
hatch 107, 111.
hatchback 92.
hazelnut 46.
head 11, 24, 25, 26, 32, 39, 75, 76, 114, 116, 131.
head linesman 120.
head of sail 136.
headband 86, 131, 133.
headboard 62.
headland 13.
headlight 90, 95, 100, 111.
headlight/turn signal 91.
headlights 92.
headphone 86.
headphone jack 86.
heads 75.
hearing, organ of 35.
heart 140.
heartwood 18.
heat shield 107.
heater controls 91.
hedge 51.
hedge trimmer 52.
heel 32, 78, 114, 123, 127.
heel piece 132.
height-adjustment lever 53.
helicopter 105.
helium sphere 106.
helix 35.
helmet 108, 121, 127.
hen 50.
hen house 49.
high beam 92.
high-speed train 100.
highlighter pen 72.
hill 14.
hind leg 24, 25, 27.
hind toe 22, 23.
hind wing 24, 25.
hinge 57, 144.
hip 32.
hip pad 121.
hip pad girdle 127.
hipbone 33.
hitting area 123.
hive 25.
hive body 25.
hock 20, 21.
hockey 125.
hockey skate 128.
hockey, ball 125.
hockey, field 125.
hoisting block 148.

hoisting rope 77, 148.
home plate 122.
honeybee 25.
honeycomb 25.
hood 90, 135.
hoof 20.
hook 57, 128, 143, 148.
hooker 119.
hopper car 101.
horizontal stabilizer 105.
horn 91, 94, 147.
horns 26.
horny beak 28.
hors d'oeuvre dish 64.
horse 20.
horseradish 40.
hose 146.
hose nozzle 53.
hose trolley 53.
hospital 152.
hot pepper 42.
hourglass 141.
house 55.
house, exterior of a 56.
housing 76.
hub 98.
hubcap 90.
huckleberry 44.
human denture 34.
humerus 33.
husk 39.
hut 54.
hydrant intake 147.
hydraulic jack 93.
hydraulic shovel 151.

I

ice cream spoon 66.
ice cube tray 70.
ice dispenser 96.
ice hockey 126, 127.
ice hockey player 127.
igloo 54.
ignition switch 91.
image sensor 89.
in goal 119.
incandescent lamp 63.
incisors 34.
incoming message cassette 85.
index finger 36.
Indian chapati bread 37.
Indian fig 45.
Indian naan bread 37.
Indian Ocean 12.
indicators 88.
indigo 71.
indoor games 140.
infield 122.
inflorescent vegetables 41.
informations 152.
inhaul 136.
inner bark 18.
inner table 140.
inner tent 138.
insect-eating bird 23.
inside 65.
inside left 118.
inside linebacker 120.
inside right 118.
inside-leg snap-fastening 83.
instrument board 91.
instrument board 91.
instrument unit 106.
internal frame 139.
internode 16.
Io 9.
iris 35.
Irish soda bread 37.
isba 54.

J

J-2 engine 106.
Jack 140.
jacket 82.
jalousie 57.
jamb 57.
Japanese persimmon 45.
Japanese plum 43.
jaw 76.

jeans 83.
jersey 121.
Jerusalem artichoke 40.
Jewish hallah bread 37.
jib 148.
jib tie 148.
jockey roller 99.
Joker 140.
Jupiter 9.

K

kangaroo 30.
kernel 39.
kerosene tank 106.
key 113, 115.
key bed 113.
key signature 112.
keyboard 74, 113.
keyboard cable 74.
King 140.
kiosk 96.
kitchen timer 141.
kitchen utensils 66.
kiwi 45.
knee 20, 31.
knee pad 121, 123, 127.
knee sock 133.
kneecap 33.
knife 65.
knife 135.
knit shirt 81.
knob 123.
knurled bolt 77.
kohlrabi 40.
kumquat 44.

L

labial palp 24.
lace 123.
ladder 93, 151.
ladder pipe nozzle 146.
ladle 66.
lagoon 13.
lake 14.
lamb 50.
lamp 144.
landing 58.
landing light 105.
lane 134.
lane number 134.
lane rope 134.
lantern 51.
lanyard 141.
lapel 80.
large blade 139.
last quarter 10.
launch escape system 106.
lava flow 13.
lava layer 13.
lawn 51.
lawn edger 52.
lawn mower 53.
lawn rake 52.
lead 72.
leaf 16, 39, 60.
leaf vegetables 38.
leaf, parts of a 17.
leafstalk 17.
leather skin 124.
ledger lines 112.
leech 136.
leek 41.
left back 118, 125.
left center 119.
left cornerback 120.
left defense 126.
left defensive end 120.
left defensive tackle 120.
left field 122.
left fielder 122.
left forward 129.
left guard 120, 129.
left half 118, 125.
left halfback 120.
left inner 125.
left safety 120.
left service court 130.
left tackle 120.
left wing 119, 125, 126.

leg 22, 28, 32, 53, 60, 62, 116.
legs 24.
lemon 44.
length, measure of 143.
lens 87.
lens hood 89.
lentils 39.
leveling-adjustment foot 87.
lever 68, 96, 146.
license plate light 92.
lid 67, 68.
lifeboat 102.
lift arm 150.
lift-arm cylinder 150.
ligature 115.
light 135, 145.
light bar 147.
lighting cable 93.
lightning 15.
lightning rod 56.
lights 63.
limb 18, 137.
limousine 92.
line 112.
line judge 120.
line of scrimmage 120.
linen 62.
linesman 118, 126, 130.
lining 78, 83.
lion 29.
lip 20, 21.
liquid hydrogen tank 106.
liquid oxygen tank 106.
liquid-crystal display 141.
listen button 85.
litchi 45.
Little Bear 11.
little finger 36.
little finger hook 115.
livestock car 101.
living room 138.
load backrest 148.
loading gate 110.
lobate toe 23.
lobe 23, 35.
lobster 26.
lock 99.
lock 57.
lock forward 119.
lock rail 57.
lock ring 87.
locking device 77.
loins 20, 32.
long-range jet 104.
lookout tower 55.
loophole 55.
loose-leaf filler 73.
loudspeaker 89.
loudspeaker 147.
lounge 102.
love seat 61.
low beam 92.
lower cannon 108.
lower chord 97.
lower eyelid 27, 35.
lower lip 34.
lower rudder 103.
luff 136.
lug 116.
luggage rack 93.
lunar module 106.
lunule 36.

M

machete 109.
machine gun 111.
machinery store 49.
magazine 110.
magazine base 110.
magazine catch 110.
magma 13.
magma chamber 13.
magnetic gasket 70.
magnifier 139.
main engines 107.
main landing gear 104.
main mirror 145.
main stand 95.

The terms in **bold type** indicate the title of an illustration.

main tube 145.
main vent 13.
maintenance 96.
mallet 75.
mallet 116.
mandarin 44.
mandible 24, 25, 27.
mane 20.
maneuvering engine 107.
mango 43.
manual focusing knob 87.
margin 17.
marker light 94.
marker pen 72.
Mars 9.
mars light 146.
mask 123, 135.
mast 136.
mast foot 136.
mast sleeve 136.
masthead 136.
material handling 148.
mattress 62.
mattress cover 62.
maxilla 27.
meadow 49.
measure of distance 143.
measure of length 143.
measure of temperature 143.
measure of time 141.
measure of weight 142.
measuring cap 68.
measuring spoons 66.
meat keeper 70.
mechanical pencil 72.
mechanical stage 144.
mechanical stage control 144.
mechanics 96.
Mediterranean Sea 12.
memo book 73.
memo pad 73.
memory cancel 74.
memory recall 74.
men 140.
men's clothing 79, 80.
Mercury 9.
mercury bulb 143.
mercury column 143.
merlon 55.
message time selector 85.
metacarpal bone 33.
metal frame 113.
metatarsal bone 33.
microcomputer 74.
microphone 89.
microprocessor 74.
middle finger 36.
middle leg 24, 25.
middle linebacker 120.
middle sole 78.
midrange 89.
midrange pickup 116.
midrib 17.
milk bread 37.
Milky Way 11.
minivan 92.
minute hand 141.
mirror 59, 95.
missile 103.
missile tube 103.
mist 15.
mixing bowl 68.
moat 55.
mode selectors 86.
molars 34.
Moon 9.
Moon, phases of the 10.
morel 19.
motor 53, 95.
motor unit 68.
motorcycle 95.
motorhome 93.
mound 122.
mountain 14.
mountain slope 14.
mountain torrent 14.
mounting bracket 137.

mounting foot 87.
mouse 74.
mouth 26, 27, 34.
mouthpiece 115, 135.
movable jaw 76.
movie theater 102.
mud flap 94.
Muenster 47.
muffler felt 113.
muffler pedal 113.
multiply key 74.
multipurpose vehicle 92.
muntin 57.
mushroom, parts of a 19.
musical notation 112.
muskmelon 42.
mustache 22.
muzzle 20, 21, 110.

nail 75.
nail file 139.
nail nick 139.
name plate 76.
nape 22, 32.
natural 112.
natural arch 13.
navel 31.
navigation light 104.
nebula 11.
neck 20, 28, 31, 65, 114, 141.
neckroll 62.
necktie 80.
nectarine 43.
Neptune 9.
net 130.
net 129.
net band 130.
net judge 130.
neutral zone 120.
new crescent 10.
new moon 10.
newel post 58.
nipple 31.
no entry 152.
no parking 152.
no smoking 152.
no. 8 forward 119.
nock 137.
nocking point 137.
node 16.
nonstriker 124.
North America 12.
North Star 11.
nose 20, 36, 104.
nose landing gear 104.
nose leather 21.
nose of the quarter 78.
nosepad 84.
nostril 20, 22, 27, 28, 36.
notch 80.
note book 73.
note symbols 112.
nozzle 146.
nozzle 106, 146, 147.
nucleus 11.
number key 74.
numeric keyboard 142.
nut 76, 109, 114.
nuts 46.

objective 144.
objective lens 144, 145.
oboe 117.
observation window 107.
Oceania 12.
octave mechanism 115.
odometer 91.
offensive 120.
office 96.
officials' bench 126.
oil warning light 91.
okra 42.
old crescent 10.
olive 43.
on-deck circle 122.
on/off 86.

on/off light 85.
on/off switch 74, 85.
on/off/volume 86.
one-way traffic 152.
open-air terrace 102.
operator's cab 148.
orange 44, 71.
orchard 49.
orchestra 117.
ostrich 30.
outdoor light 56.
outer bark 18.
outer table 140.
outfield 122.
outhaul 136.
outlet 93.
output jack 116.
outrigger 146, 148, 151.
outside left 118.
outside linebacker 120.
outside mirror 90.
outside right 118.
outsole 78.
ovary 17.
oven 69.
oven control knob 69.
overall 83.
overcoat 82.
overflow 59.
overpass 97.
ovule 17.
ox 50.

Pacific Ocean 12.
packsack 139.
pad 21.
paint roller 77.
painting upkeep 77.
paling fence 51.
palm 36, 123.
palmette 61.
pan 142.
pane 57.
panel 57.
pantograph 100.
pants 80.
pants 121, 123, 127.
papaya 45.
paper clips 72.
parallelepiped 71.
parallelogram 71.
parapet 97.
parapet walk 55.
parking brake lever 91.
Parmesan 47.
parsnip 40.
pass 14.
passenger cabin 104.
passenger liner 102.
pastern 20.
patch pocket 83.
patera 61.
path 51.
patio 51.
pauldron 108.
pause/still 88.
payload 106.
payload bay door 107.
peach 43.
peak 14, 79.
peanut 46.
pear 43.
pecan nut 46.
pectoral fin 27.
pedal 98, 99, 116.
pedal rod 113.
pedestal 96.
pedestrian crossing 152.
pedicel 17.
pedometer 143.
peg 114, 138.
peg box 114.
peg nut 138.
pen blade 139.
penalty arc 118.
penalty area 118.
penalty bench 126.

penalty spot 118.
pencil 72.
pencil sharpener 73.
penis 31.
pepper shaker 64.
percent key 74.
perching bird 23.
pergola 51.
periscope 103.
periscopic sight 111.
permanent pasture 49.
perpetual snows 14.
perron 56.
personal articles 84.
petals 17.
Petit Suisse 47.
phases of the Moon 10.
philtrum 36.
Phobos 9.
photoelectric cell 87.
piano 117.
piccolo 117.
pick guard 116.
pickling onion 41.
pickup selector 116.
pickup truck 92.
pie 48.
pier 97.
pig 50.
piggyback car 101.
pigsty 49.
pile dwelling 54.
pillow 62.
pillow case 62.
pillow protector 62.
pillow sham 62.
pilot 100.
pin 146.
pin block 113.
pine nut 46.
pineapple 45.
pip 140.
pistachio nut 46.
pistil 17.
pistol 110.
pistol grip handle 76.
pit 28.
pita bread 37.
pitch 124.
pitcher 122.
pitcher's plate 122.
pith 18.
pivot 128.
pivot cab 151.
plane surfaces 71.
planets of the solar system 9.
plant, parts of a 16.
plastron 28.
plateau 14.
platform 77, 142.
platform ladder 77.
platter 64.
play 88.
play button 86.
player's number 121.
player's stick 127.
players' bench 122, 126, 129.
playroom 102.
pleasure garden 51.
pleated skirt 82.
plug 76.
plum 43.
Pluto 9.
pocket 83.
pocket calculator 74.
pocket handkerchief 80.
point 65, 114, 128, 137, 140.
pointer 142, 143.
poison 152.
poisonous mushroom 19.
polar bear 30.
polar lights 11.
pole grip 132, 133.
pole shaft 133.
pole tip 133.
poleyn 108.
pollen basket 25.

The terms in **bold type** indicate the title of an illustration.

pome fruits 43.
pomegranate 45.
poniard 109.
pool 51.
popping crease 124.
port 102.
port sail plane 103.
portable cellular telephone 85.
portable shower head 59.
porthole 102.
position marker 114, 116.
potato 40.
potato masher 66.
pothole 14.
poulaine 108.
power car 100.
power cord 53.
power switch 87, 88.
power train 99.
power-off slide-select bar 87.
premolars 34.
preset buttons 88.
pressure bar 113.
pressure cooker 67.
pressure gauge 146.
pressure regulator 67.
price per litre/gallon 96.
primary root 16.
printed document 74.
printer 74.
prism 71.
proboscis 24.
process Emmenthal 47.
process Gruyère 47.
processed cheese 47.
product codes 142.
profiterole 48.
prolegs 24.
promenade deck 102.
prominence 10.
prong 65.
prop forward 119.
prop stand 95.
propane cylinder 93.
propeller 102, 103.
protective cup 121, 127.
protective helmet 99.
pubis 31.
public signs 152.
puck 127.
pulley 77, 109.
pulley block 109.
pulmonary opening 26.
pulse button 68.
pump island 96.
pump nozzle 96.
pumper 147.
pumpernickel bread 37.
pumpkin 42.
punch hole 78.
pupil 35.
purfling 114.
purge valve 135.
push buttons 85.
push-button 72.
push-button telephone 85.
pyramid 71.

quarter 78.
quarter note 112.
quarter rest 112.
quarterback 120.
Queen 140.
queen excluder 25.
quince 43.

rack 67, 69.
radar 104.
radar antenna 102, 103.
radiation zone 10.
radiator fan 100.
radiator grill 94.
radicle 16.
radio antenna 103.
radish 40.
radius 33.
raglan sleeve 79.

rail 100.
rain 15.
rainbow 15.
raindrop 15.
rainfly 138.
rake 52.
ramekin 64.
rampart 55.
rapier 109.
reactor 103.
reactor deck 103.
rear brake 98.
rear derailleur 98, 99.
rear headlights 92.
rear leg 60.
rear light 98.
rear sight 110.
rearview mirror 91.
receiver 130.
receptacle 17.
record 88.
record button 89.
recorder power switch 88.
rectangle 71.
red 71.
red rind 47.
Red Sea 12.
reed 115.
referee 118, 120, 126, 129.
reflecting telescope 145.
refracting telescope 145.
refrigerator 70.
refrigerator car 101.
refrigerator compartment 70.
release button 87.
remote control 88.
remote control 87.
remote control detector 88.
remote control terminal 87.
remote-control arm 107.
removable blade 77.
reservoir 68.
reset button 141.
rest symbols 112.
restaurant 152.
restricted area 129.
restricting circle 129.
retractable entry step 93.
return crease 124.
reverse slide change 87.
revolver 110.
revolving nosepiece 144.
rewind 88.
rewind button 86.
rhinoceros 29.
rhombus 71.
rhubarb 39.
rib 33, 39, 84, 114, 151.
rib pad 121.
ribbing 81, 83.
Ricotta 47.
ridge 14.
right back 118, 125.
right center 119.
right cornerback 120.
right defense 126.
right defensive end 120.
right defensive tackle 120.
right field 122.
right fielder 122.
right forward 129.
right guard 120, 129.
right half 118, 125.
right halfback 120.
right inner 125.
right safety 120.
right service court 130.
right tackle 120.
right turn 152.
right wing 119, 125, 126.
rim 84, 95, 98, 129.
rim soup bowl 64.
rinceau 61.
ring 19, 84, 115, 139.
ring binder 73.
ringer selector 85.

rink 126.
rink corner 126.
ripper 149.
ripper cylinder 149.
ripper tip 149.
ripper tooth 149.
riser 58.
river estuary 13.
rivet 128.
road signs, major 152.
roasting pans 67.
Roberval's balance 142.
rock 13.
rock garden 51.
rocket 106.
roller cover 77.
roller frame 77.
roller skate 128.
roof 25, 56.
roof air conditioner 93.
roof vent 56, 93.
room 138.
room thermostat 143.
rooster 50.
root 16.
root 16, 65.
root cap 16.
root hairs 16.
root of nose 36.
root vegetables 40.
root-hair zone 18.
roots 18.
rose 53.
rosette 114.
rotating sprinkler 53.
rotor blade 105.
rotor head 105.
rotor hub 105.
rudder 102, 104, 107.
rugby 119.
rugby, ball 119.
rugby, field 119.
ruler 72.
ruler 139.
run 124.
rung 77.
runner 140.
running shoe 78.
Russian pumpernickel bread 37.
rutabaga 40.

saber 109.
saddle 98.
safety chain 93.
safety rail 77, 100.
safety valve 67.
sail 136.
sailboard 136.
salad bowl 64.
salad plate 64.
salad spinner 66.
salsify 40.
salt marsh 13.
salt shaker 64.
sand 141.
sand island 13.
sapwood 18.
sash-frame 57.
Saturn 9.
saucepan 67.
saucer 64.
saxophone 115.
scale 112.
scale 23, 27, 28, 143.
scallion 41.
Scandinavian crak bread 37.
school 152.
school supplies 72, 73.
scissors 139.
sconce 63.
scorer 129.
scraper 77.
screen 88.
screen print 83.
screen window 138.
screw 75.
screw 114.

screw base 63.
screwdriver 75.
screwdriver 139.
scroll 114.
scroll foot 61.
scrum half 119.
seal 30.
seam 79, 124.
seat 60, 61.
seat cover 59.
seat post 98.
seat-belt warning light 91.
second base 122.
second baseman 122.
second dorsal fin 27.
second floor 56.
second hand 141.
second space 129.
second stage 106.
second violin 117.
secondary root 16.
seed leaf 16.
seed vegetables 39.
seed-eating bird 23.
segment score number 137.
semicircle 129.
semitrailer 94.
sepals 17.
server 130.
service line 130.
service module 106.
service station 96.
service station 152.
serving bowl 64.
sesame seeded pita bread 37.
set of coloring pencils 73.
set of utensils 66.
set-in sleeve 81, 83.
sewn-in floor 138.
sex 31.
shade 63.
shadow 141.
shaft 127, 131, 137.
shallot 41.
shank 75, 84.
shank protector 149.
sharp 112.
sheath 17, 21.
shed 51.
sheep 50.
sheep shelter 49.
shelf 70, 77.
shelf channel 70.
shell 26, 28.
sherbet 48.
shield 28, 90.
shifter 98, 99.
shin guard 121, 123.
shin pad 127.
shinbone 33.
shirt 83.
shirt 80.
shirt cuff 80.
shirttail 80.
shock absorber 95.
shoelace 78.
shoot 16, 18.
shooting star 11.
shortstop 122.
shoulder 20, 21, 31, 131.
shoulder blade 32, 33.
shoulder pad 121, 127.
shoulder strap 84, 139.
shovel 52, 132, 133.
shower head 59.
shower stall 59.
shutter 57.
sickle 52.
side 65.
side chair 60.
side compression strap 139.
side rail 77.
side span 97.
side vent 13, 93.
side wall 134.
side-marker light 92.
sideline 125, 129.

The terms in **bold type** indicate the title of an illustration.

sight 137.
sight, organ of 35.
signal lamp 67, 68, 69.
silverware 65.
simple eye 24, 25.
simple-span beam bridge 97.
single-breasted coat 80.
single-breasted coat 80.
singles pole 130.
singles sideline 130.
sink 59.
sinkhole 14.
siphon 14.
sixteenth note 112.
sixteenth rest 112.
sixty-fourth note 112.
sixty-fourth rest 112.
skate 127.
skating 128.
skeg 136.
skeleton 33.
ski boot 132.
ski goggles 132.
ski hat 132, 133.
ski pole 132, 133.
ski stop 132.
ski suit 132, 133.
ski tip 133.
skid 105.
skimmer 66.
skin 27.
skin diving 135.
skirt 131.
skirts 82.
skull 33.
skylight 56.
sleeper 83.
sleeper-cab 94.
sleeping bag 139.
sleeve strap 79.
sleeve strap loop 79.
slide 87, 110.
slide projector 87.
slide tray 87.
sliding roof 90.
slip joint 76.
slip joint pliers 76.
slit 79.
slot 65, 68, 75.
slow-motion 88.
smell, organ of 36.
smoke-grenade launcher 111.
snail 26.
snap fastener 80.
snap-fastening front 83.
snare 116.
snare drum 116.
snare drum 117.
snare head 116.
snare strainer 116.
snorkel 135.
snorkel exhaust 103.
snorkel intake 103.
snout 27.
snow 15.
snow crystals 15.
soap dish 59.
soccer 118.
soccer ball 118.
soccer, field 118.
sock 121, 131.
sofa 61.
soft cheese 47.
soft palate 34.
soft pedal 113.
soft ray 27.
soft-drink dispenser 96.
solar cell 74.
solar spectrum 71.
solar system, planets of the 9.
sole 128.
sole plate 128.
solid body 116.
solids 71.
solleret 108.
soufflé 48.

sound hole 114.
sound reproducing system 89.
soundboard 113, 114.
soup bowl 64.
soup tureen 64.
South America 12.
Southern Cross 11.
sow 50.
soybeans 39.
space 112.
space shuttle 107.
spacelab 107.
spade 52, 140.
Spanish onion 41.
spatula 66.
speaker 85, 86.
speaker volume control 85.
speed control 68.
speed limit 152.
speed skate 128.
speedometer 91.
sphere 71.
spicules 10.
spiked shoe 123.
spinach 38.
spindle 60.
spiny ray 27.
spiracle 24.
spit 13.
splat 61.
split end 120.
spoiler 95.
spoke 98.
spoon 65.
spores 19.
sports car 92.
spotlight 146, 147.
spreader 84.
sprocket wheel 111, 149.
spur 14, 116.
square 71.
square cushion 62.
square root key 74.
stabilizer 137.
stabilizer fin 102.
stabilizing fin 106.
stack 13.
staff 112.
stage 144.
stage clip 144.
stairs 58.
stake 51.
stalactite 14.
stalagmite 14.
stalk 39.
stalk vegetables 39.
stamen 17.
stanchion 128.
stand 63, 68, 116.
standoff half 119.
stapler 73.
staples 73.
starboard 102.
starboard diving plane 103.
stars 11.
start button 141.
starting block 134.
starting step 58.
stateroom 102.
station wagon 92.
steering column 91.
steering wheel 91.
stem 16.
stem 16, 19, 98, 143.
step 58, 77, 94, 100.
step setting 143.
stepladder 77.
stereo control 86.
stern 102, 136.
stern deck 102.
stick 125.
stick 114, 116, 127.
stick eraser 72.
stick glove 127.
stiffening girder 97.
stigma 17.
stile 57, 60.

Stilton 47.
sting 25.
stipule 17.
stirrup 109.
stirrup sock 123.
stitch 78.
stitches 123.
stitching 79.
stock pot 67.
stone fruits 43.
stool 57.
stop 21, 88, 152.
stop button 141.
stoplight 92.
stopwatch 141.
storage compartment 87, 93, 94, 146, 147.
storage door 70.
straight skirt 82.
strainer 138.
strap 83, 123.
strap loop 139.
stretcher 60.
striker 124.
striking circle 125.
string 114.
stringer 58.
stringing 131.
strings 113.
stud 78.
stump 18.
stump 124.
style 17.
submarine 103.
submersible watch 135.
subterranean stream 14.
subtract from memory 74.
subtract key 74.
suction hose 147.
sugar bowl 64.
sugar peas 39.
summer squash 42.
summit 14.
Sun 10.
Sun 9.
sun viser 91, 93.
sun's atmosphere 10.
sun's surface 10.
sundeck 102.
sundial 141.
sunglasses 84.
sunspot 10.
super 25.
support 60, 63, 145.
support leg 93.
surface element 69.
surface of the water 134.
suspended span 97.
suspender 97.
suspension bridge 97.
suspension cable 97.
swallow hole 14.
sweaters 81.
sweet pepper 42.
sweet potato 40.
swimming 134.
swimming legs 26.
swimming pool 134.
swimming pool 102.
swing circle 151.
Swiss chard 39.
Swiss knife 139.
Swiss roll 48.
switch 68, 76.
switch lock 76.
swivel head 76.

T-shirt 83.
tab 84.
table lamp 63.
table mixer 68.
tack 136.
tag 78.
tail 20, 21, 22, 27, 28, 104, 132, 133.
tail boom 105.
tail fan 26.
taillight 92, 95.
tailpiece 114.

talon 23.
tang 65.
tank 111.
tank car 101.
tank lid 59.
tanks 107.
tap connector 53.
tape 123, 125, 143.
tape lock 143.
tape measure 143.
taproot 18.
tarsal bone 33.
tart 48.
tasset 108.
taste, organ of 34.
team shirt 123.
teapot 64.
teeth 75.
telephone 152.
telephone set 85.
telephone/answering system 85.
telescopic boom 148.
telescopic front fork 95.
television set 88.
temperature control 68.
temperature indicator 91.
temperature set point knob 143.
temperature, measure of 143.
temple 84.
tendon guard 128.
tennis 130, 131.
tennis ball 131.
tennis player 131.
tennis racket 131.
tennis shoe 131.
tenor drum 116.
tension rod 116.
tension roller 99.
tension screw 116.
tent 138.
tepee 54.
terminal bud 16.
thermometer 143.
thermostat 67.
thermostat control 70.
thigh 20, 21, 32.
thigh pad 121.
thighbone 33.
third base 122.
third baseman 122.
third finger 36.
third stage 106.
thirty-second note 112.
thirty-second rest 112.
thorax 24, 31.
thread 75.
threaded rod 76.
three-quarter backs 119.
threshold 57.
throat 22, 76, 131.
throat protector 123, 127.
thrust 97.
thrusting weapons 109.
thumb 36, 79, 123.
thumb hook 115.
thumb rest 115.
thumb tacks 73.
thumbscrew 76.
ticket 142.
tie 100.
tie closure 84.
tie plate 100.
tight end 120.
tightening buckle 139.
tiller 109.
tilt-back head 68.
time signature 112.
time, measure of 141.
timed outlet 69.
timekeeper 129.
timer 67.
timpani 117.
tinted lens 84.
tip 17, 26, 39, 65, 75, 84, 132.
tip of nose 36.
tire 98.
tire inflator 96.

The terms in **bold type** indicate the title of an illustration.

tire pump 98.
tire valve 98.
tissue holder 59.
Titan 9.
toaster 68.
toe 21, 22, 23, 31, 75.
toe box 128.
toe clip 98.
toe picks 128.
toe piece 132.
toe stop 128.
toilet 59.
toilet bowl 59.
toilet tank 59.
toilets 152.
tomato 42.
tomme au raisin 47.
tone control 116.
tone controls 86.
tongs 66.
tongue 28, 34, 78, 128.
tongue sheath 28.
tonsil 34.
tool tray 77.
tools 52, 53, 76.
tooth 28, 34, 151.
top 18.
top collar 80.
top flap 139.
top ladder 146.
top rail 57.
top stitching 83.
torpedo 103.
torpedo room 103.
total 142.
touch line 118, 119.
touch, organ of 36.
towbar 93.
towel bar 59.
tower 97.
tower crane 148.
tower ladder 146.
tower mast 148.
tower silo 49.
towing hitch 93.
track 149.
track light 63.
track link 111.
track shoe 111.
tractor 94, 150.
traditional houses 54.
traffic lights 152.
trailer 93.
trailer 100.
trapezoid 71.
tray 53, 77, 145.
treble pickup 116.
tree, parts of a 18.
trench coat 79.
triangle 72.
triangle 71, 117.
trigger 89, 109, 110.
trigger guard 110.
trip odometer 91.
triple ring 137.
tripod 145.
tripod stand 116.
Triton 9.
trolley 148.
trombone 117.

tropical fruits 45.
truck 100, 128.
truck crane 148.
truck frame 100.
truck tractor 94.
truck trailer 94.
trumpet 115.
trumpet 117.
trunk 18, 32, 90.
trunk, cross section of a 18.
tub 51.
tub platform 59.
tuba 117.
tuber vegetables 40.
tubular bells 117.
tuning machine 116.
tuning pin 113.
tuning slide 115.
tuning switch 86.
tunnel 107.
turbine 103.
turbojet engine 104.
turkey 50.
turn signal 92, 95.
turner 66.
turning wall 134.
turnip 40.
turnover 48.
turntable 68, 89.
turntable mounting 146.
turret 111.
turtle 28.
turtleneck 81.
turtleneck 133.
TV power switch 88.
TV/video button 88.
tweeter 89.
twig 16, 18.
two-door sedan 92.
two-handed sword 109.
two-way collar 79.
type of fuel 96.

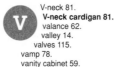

ulna 33.
umbrella 84.
umpire 120, 130.
umpire-in-chief 122.
underpass 97.
undershirt 123.
unit price 142.
unleavened bread 37.
unripened cheese 47.
uphaul 136.
upper cannon 108.
upper chord 97.
upper deck 104.
upper eyelid 27, 35.
upper lip 34.
upper rudder 103.
upright piano 113.
Uranus 9.
uvula 34.

V-neck 81.
V-neck cardigan 81.
valance 62.
valley 14.
valves 115.
vamp 78.
vanity cabinet 59.

vanity mirror 91.
vegetable bowl 64.
vegetable garden 49.
vegetable steamer 67.
vein 17.
Velcro® closure 84.
venom canal 28.
venom fang 28.
venom gland 28.
venomous snake 28.
vent 91.
ventral fin 27.
Venus 9.
vertebra 33.
vertical pupil 28.
vest 81.
vest 80.
vibrato arm 116.
video camera 89.
videocassette recorder 88.
Vienna bread 37.
vine leaf 38.
vinyl grip sole 83.
viola 117.
violet 71.
violin 114.
vision slit 108.
volcanic bombs 13.
volcano 13.
volume control 86, 88, 116.
volume readout 96.
volva 19.

wading bird 23.
waffle 48.
waist 32.
waist belt 139.
waistband 80, 83.
waistband extension 80.
walking legs 26.
wall 138.
wallet 84.
walnut 46.
warming plate 68.
warning lights 91.
warning plate 76.
watch pocket 80.
water bottle 98.
water bottle clip 98.
water key 115.
water level 68.
water pitcher 64.
water pressure gauge 147.
water table 14.
watercolor paints 73.
watercress 38.
waterfall 14.
watering can 53.
watermelon 42.
weather 15.
weatherboard 57.
web 23, 27, 123.
webbed toe 23, 27.
weighing platform 142.
weight 142.
weight belt 135.
weight, measure of 142.
welt pocket 81.
wet suit 135.
wheel 53, 90, 111, 128, 137.

wheel loader 150.
wheelbarrow 53.
whiskers 21.
white 35, 140.
white cabbage 38.
white light 71.
white rind 47.
white-tailed deer 30.
whole meal bread 37.
whole note 112.
whole rest 112.
whole wheat bread 37.
whorl 26.
wicket 124.
wicketkeeper 124.
wigwam 54.
wild animals 29, 30.
willow 124.
wind deflector 94.
windbreaker 80.
window 57.
window 69, 90, 104, 136.
window canopy 138.
windshield 90, 95.
windshield wiper 90.
wing 22, 24, 104, 107.
wing vein 24.
wiper switch 91.
wire cutter 76.
wisdom tooth 34.
wishbone boom 136.
withers 20, 21.
women's clothing 82.
wood ray 18.
woofer 89.
wrap-over top 82.
wrist 21, 32, 36.
wrist strap 132, 133.
wristband 131.

xylophone 117.

yellow 71.
yield 152.
yule log 48.
yurt 54.

zebra 29.
zipper 138.
zoom adjustment 144.
zoom lens 89.
zoom lever 89.
zucchini 42.